FinFit

JARHRO PUBLISHING

ISBN: 978-0-646-99640-0 (print), 978-0-646-99641-7 (epub)

FinFit

Your Ultimate Financial Fitness Training Guide

PHIL SGANGARELLA
DONNA SGANGARELLA

To our three boys Jarrod, Rhys and Rocco,
everything we do, we do for you.

Disclaimer

The purpose of this book is to provide the reader with general direction on how best to arrange their financial affairs. Nothing within this book constitutes personal or even general financial product advice or personal or general class of product advice. The reader should be aware before reading this book that any reliance on anything said in it to make a personal financial decision about a particular financial product or a class of financial products is done at the reader's sole risk and should not be done in the absence of personal advice from an investment or insurance professional.

Contents

Introduction

Thank you for reading our book. We are so excited to share with you our ideas and strategies to help you become financially fit.

We are Phil and Donna Sgangarella, the founders of FinFit Wealth Solutions—a *one-stop-shop* for all your wealth needs. We have clients all over Australia, and the focus and goal of our business is to help our clients become financially fit (FinFit for short).

Neither of us came from wealthy families.

Phil's parents immigrated from Italy to Australia in 1960. They settled in Wollongong in New South Wales and set about creating a foundation for the family so they could make Australia their home. They wanted to make sure their children had the opportunity to succeed. For Phil, the circumstances his family experienced in the early years, as migrants, fuelled his desire to make sure that he had something to show for the years he knew he would have to work when he left school. When he started earning money, he got into the habit of saving. His first job wasn't in financial services, it was in information technology. After four years, he had saved enough to go on a three-month European holiday. By the time he was 21, he had enough of a deposit to buy his own home. This gave him a real launchpad into the world of investing as, before the age of 30, he was able to purchase two investment properties with the equity that had built up in his home and the savings he had in his bank account. His own personal experiences with saving and investing drove his desire to move into financial services. He started his financial planning career at the age of 32 and moved to Sydney.

Donna grew up on a tomato farm in Bundaberg, Queensland. Her weekends were spent in a tomato shed helping her family pack tomatoes. She had a passion for finance from a very young age. She applied for her first job at the age of 13 (so she didn't have to pack tomatoes every weekend!) and started saving her money. She worked in a fruit shop and saved every dollar she earned. The money in her savings account increased steadily, and this inspired her to work more and save more, as she wanted to be able to buy a car when she was old enough to get her licence.

She proudly paid cash for her first car.

Her focus then moved onto saving for her first home. Donna worked two jobs and saved everything. While her friends were travelling and clubbing, she would limit her spending to save for her goal.

Donna started her career as a receptionist in a Bundaberg legal firm. She loved her job as she could talk to people all day long and she learned so much. She was offered a job in Sydney by one of the firm's major clients, and she jumped at the opportunity. She was a 17-year-old Bundy girl who had never left Queensland.

At that time, she had no idea that her move to Sydney would change her life forever.

Donna was fortunate to have close friends in Sydney that offered her accommodation while she established herself. They were the only people she knew when she moved.

Her career skyrocketed and at the age of 20 she was offered a job at Westpac Bank. She started as the assistant to the branch manager and was then promoted to be a financial planner thanks to her knowledge, relationship skills, and determination. She then studied financial planning and realised she had been personally working with the fundamentals of financial planning without realising it. This then drove Donna to help other people improve their financial lives.

Donna bought her first home at 21.

Years later our worlds collided, and it was love at first sight.

We now use our personal life experiences, along with our personal qualifications as a Certified Financial Planner and as a Mortgage Broker, and also our over 35 years' combined experience in the finance industry to provide personal financial coaching services to our clients.

We are happily married with three healthy boys—Jarrod who was born in 1998, Rhys who was born in 2001, and Rocco who was born in 2012.

We have our own home (with a mortgage), a portfolio of shares and investment properties, and we clear our credit card each month. This has not happened overnight; it has taken years of hard work and focus to reach different levels of the ladder on the way to financial fitness.

One of our goals has been to write a book to educate Australians when it comes to improving their financial position and living the life they want to live.

We want to share with you the things we have done personally to reach *our* financial fitness goals, and share examples of strategies we've used with our clients to improve *their* financial fitness.

We want you to think differently about your financial situation, and we want you to think about the financial decisions you're about to make *before* you make them.

We want you to be financially fit!

CHAPTER 1

From Financially Flabby to Lean Mean Money-Making Machine

It's time to work smarter, not harder, to reach peak financial fitness.

We both have the same vision when it comes to our future, and that is:

> *"In the future, at a time of our choosing, we are going to be financially independent."*

We are not going to achieve this vision if we have no goals, are not saving money, and have too much bad debt.

What you want to consider is:

> *What do I need to do now to put myself in a better financial position in the future?*

Financial matters can be confusing, and most people don't know where to start.

This book will give you the guidance you need to become financially fit. We'll show you where to start, and what to do next.

We want you to put these concepts and ideas into practice. We'll guide you through a self-assessment, a financial health check that will enable you to determine your current financial fitness level. That way you'll know how to improve.

We'll get you lean and mean, and make you into a money-making machine!

We want you to:

- Get into the habit of checking your progress on a regular basis so you know if you are succeeding.
- Set a financial target so you can be in control of your own financial life, and become accountable to yourself.
- Analyse your spending habits so you can work out what you are spending money on. If you're not saving, you're not achieving.
- Rid yourself of your bad debt. Bad Debt is that flab around your waist that is weighing you down, and generally making you not feel good about yourself.
- Understand what your investment options are—other than just saving money in the bank, earning next to no interest, and having the tax man and inflation chew away at your savings.

Don't let an unforeseen circumstance ruin your and your family's quality of life. We'll show you what you need to consider when insuring against the probability of something going wrong. There is no room for scepticism here; having the right level of insurance is an important part of being financially fit.

We're all on the path to *financial independence*. The problem is this: not everyone spends the time working out what it will actually look like for them. They then end up being hopelessly short of where they want to be. We'll let you know what you need to consider when you're defining what *financial independence* will look like for *you*.

We'll introduce you to our **4-week FinFit Challenge**. This is the kick start you need to implement some of the concepts introduced in this book.

Then our **FinFit 90-Day Plan** will keep you focused. You will use it to achieve financial fitness, and to make sure you *stay* financially fit.

We want you to start living like you *are* financially fit, not just dreaming about it.

Also, we've injected a little fun into this book by using sporting and fitness analogies along the way. Sports and finances are similar:

- There is a goal that needs to be achieved.
- There is a plan that needs to be put into place in order to achieve that goal.
- There is a coach/mentor that will encourage you and push you along to make sure that your goal is achieved.
- There is heartbreak if that goal is not achieved.
- There is celebration when your goal is achieved!

You are the athlete and we are your coaches.

What you will read in this book works; and it will work for you.

CHAPTER 2

Your Financial Health Check

*You need to identify your problem areas
so you can work out how to improve them.*

So, you feel a little flabby around your midsection.

But you've found yourself a personal trainer, and together you will set your goals around how that flab is going to disappear!

You want to look good and feel good! Or maybe you aspire to six-pack abs!

Whatever your goal is, your first-class personal trainer will come up with a training plan for you to get those abs in shape.

Before they come up with the training plan, however, they need to understand what your base level "fitness" is. They won't put you on an advanced workout plan if you're just a beginner.

Similarly, you need to determine what base level "financial fitness" you have. And you want to identify what problem areas you have financially.

For that, you need to complete a financial health check, which is an honest self-assessment of your financially weak areas. This won't take long; it's a quick, five-minute question-and-answer session.

It will determine your base level "financial fitness," and it will identify your problem areas.

To rate yourself, fill out the following form: (This form is also available at FinFit.com.au/resources.)

Goal	No, I need help	I think so	Yes, all taken care of
I have set some financial goals that I want to achieve.			
I have extra money left over each month to put into my savings account after all my expenses are paid for.			
I understand the difference between good debt and bad debt.			
I have worked out how to repay my bad debt as quickly as possible.			
I have an investment strategy in place to help me achieve my financial goals.			
My family and I would continue to live comfortably if I became ill or was injured.			
I have a plan in place to accumulate enough funds to pay for my lifestyle when I want to be financially independent.			
I regularly review my financial situation to work out if I'm on track to achieve my goals.			

Well done! You just completed an honest self-assessment of your financial health.

How many "No! I need help" and "I think so" answers did you get? These answers tell you where you need to focus your energy. They tell you where you need to make changes to turn your financial weaknesses into your financial strengths.

How many "Yes, all taken care of" answers did you get? You might feel like you have these covered, but this book may give you a few more ideas on how to make these areas stronger.

You have two choices here:

1. You acknowledge the areas that need your attention and set about improving them.
2. You keep doing what you're doing in the hope that your problem areas will fix themselves.

We know which choice we'd make.

If you really want to succeed, read on. It will save your financial life.

We'll look at five key financial fitness areas and we'll show you ways you can improve them.

The five areas are:

1. Your financial diet – Is your financial diet on point, or are you on your way to a financial heart attack?
2. Your financial flab – Are you lean, or are you carrying extra financial weight?
3. Your financial muscles – Are you using them or losing them?
4. Your financial injury prevention – Don't let the unforeseen ruin your dreams and aspirations.
5. Your financial marathon – Are you going to go for the long haul and finish strong?

Let the journey to your financial fitness begin!

1. Financial Fitness Area: Your financial diet

Is your financial diet on point, or are you on your way to a financial heart attack?

Your financial diet is your *spending,* and it's your hard-earned dollars that you're spending.

Everyone would be financially healthier if they didn't spend money on things they don't need.

Even though that shirt, dress, or shoes are on sale, do you really need them?

"But I saved 25 percent because it was on sale!"

Yes, but you would have saved 100 percent if you didn't buy it in the first place.

You need to treat your spending just like you would your diet. Poor spending choices are the same as eating *too much junk food.* You're well on the way to a financial heart attack if you don't have control over what you spend.

2. Financial Fitness Area: Your financial flab

Are you lean, or are you carrying extra financial weight?

What do we mean by financial flab?

We're talking about **debt!**

That would be the home loan, credit card, personal loan, car loan, boat loan, bike loan, and so on.

Too much debt will create a drag on your financial fitness. It's like when you first get on the treadmill after a few months off, having put on a few kilos, and it's like you're walking into a headwind. You're puffed after five minutes!

Debt can have the same effect on your financial fitness. Every dollar you spend repaying debt is one less dollar you can spend on improving your financial wellbeing. You've got to lose all that extra weight before you can begin to see any positive results.

3. Financial Fitness Area: Your financial muscles

Are you using them or losing them?

You have a surplus of money each month, but are there options beyond just depositing it into a bank account?

What do you invest it in? For how long do you invest it?

You also need to take the right level of "risk" with your investments. If your long-term goal is to be financially independent, you may need to invest in shares and property. The more risks you take, the greater the chance of financial loss but there is also a greater chance of financial gain.

Are you taking the *right* level of risk for your situation?

Working for your money isn't the best way to achieve financial fitness. Having your money work for you is a much more efficient way of achieving financial fitness.

4. Financial Fitness Area: Your financial injury prevention

Don't let the unforeseen ruin your dreams and aspirations.

When you're working out or playing sports, you're going to get injuries. Trust us, the older you get, the more injuries you'll suffer, and you'll suffer them a lot more frequently than when you were younger.

So, what do you do when you get injured? You get treatment. Why? Because you want to get over the injury *as quickly as possible* so you can get back into what you were doing before.

People often don't *see* potential injuries that could derail their financial fitness plan.

We'll now use the word "insurance" here. We can hear the groans from readers. The fact is, people spend more on their car and home insurance than they do on their most prized asset, which is *themselves*.

Having the right *type* of insurance, as well as the right *amount* of insurance, can prevent serious financial difficulties for you and your family in case you have a major illness or injury, or worse. Having a clear plan regarding how you *fund* your insurance premiums is equally important. After all, you need to be able to pay the premiums to keep your insurance active.

5. Financial Fitness Area: Your financial marathon

Are you going to go for the long haul and finish strong?

We're all running a financial marathon. It starts when your first pay cheque hits your bank account. Everyone is at a different stage in their race.

Your financial marathon is your race to financial independence. A good marathon runner will plan their race and make sure they finish in good physical condition. You've all seen it. Those who have planned their race poorly don't finish. They are dehydrated, and they look like they need hospitalisation.

So those are your areas of financial fitness. Let's now look at what your focus is going to be. What goals do you want to achieve?

We'll show you how to set your **C.O.R.E goals**. You should now see the importance of working out your base level financial fitness. You need to identify your problem areas so you can put a plan in place to improve them.

But before we start addressing your five key financial fitness areas, there are two important foundations you need to set.

The first of these is your check point for success. You need to have a structure around how you assess whether you are on track to achieving financial fitness, and, importantly, how you make sure you *stay* financially fit once you get there.

CHAPTER 3

FinFit Friday—
Your Checkpoint for Success

*Operating without healthy communication or feedback is like driving a
car with no speedometer, cooking without ever tasting your food,
or playing football without a scoreboard.*

When you work with a personal trainer in the gym, they constantly
communicate with you about your technique, your fitness goals, the

obstacles in your way, and how you're progressing toward achieving your fitness goals.

When you're playing basketball, how do you know if you're winning? You look at the scoreboard.

The same should apply to your finances, and that is why we love FinFit Friday.

FinFit Friday is all about making time to communicate and to talk about all things finance. It's about making sure you're on track to achieve your financial fitness goals.

We love having a date and talking finance!

We review our goals on Friday night with a nice cold Sauvignon Blanc—or should we say "protein shake?"

If you're a couple, you want to be on the same page.

Imagine the sprint coach who decides he's changing his sprinter's training so he can run the 400-meter race instead of the 100-meter race. Imagine he doesn't communicate this to his sprinter. The sprinter will be focused on the 100 meters and his coach on the 400 meters. How do you think race day will go?

What should you talk about?

The agenda you set is up to you, but it should include how you are tracking to achieve your financial fitness goals.

Our agenda for our weekly FinFit Friday looks like this:

1.   What was the best thing that happened to us this week? (Yay! Cheers to that!)
2.   Goal update – How are we tracking?
3.   How much did we save this week?

4. Did we have any obstacles? If so, what do we need to change to get back on track?

5. What's the plan for next week?

We like to start our meetings with a positive, which is why we ask each other: What was the best thing that happened to us during the week? Your response doesn't have to be directly related to your financial goals. It could be anything that's made you feel good that week.

However, there does need to be some meeting preparation. You want to turn up with answers to each of your agenda items because the reason you are meeting is to make sure you're on track to achieving your financial fitness goals. The meeting would be waste of time if you didn't come prepared.

If it turns out that you are not on track regarding achieving your goals, you need to discuss a plan to get you back on track.

If you leave it too long between meetings, you run the risk of having to make bigger changes to get back on track.

FinFit Friday is equally as important if it's just *you* and you don't have a spouse or partner. You still need a regular checkpoint to determine how you are doing.

How often should you communicate?

When you're starting on your journey to financial fitness, we suggest you do this weekly.

You want to make sure you are both heading in the right direction. Until you have a consistent plan across all your trouble areas (remember the results from your health check!), you want to keep the time between FinFit Fridays as short as possible.

Once you've got your plan and your journey is in motion, you can extend the time between FinFit Fridays. At that point we suggest you meet at least monthly.

How long should you meet for?

Regardless of whether you're having your catch-up over a glass at wine at home or you decide to go out to a restaurant for dinner, don't drag this on.

Who likes a long meeting anyway? You start to lose focus if you let the meeting drag on.

We can go through our four agenda items in 15 minutes, and then we can have our dinner and discuss anything else, like the kids, family, and friends.

You should be able to discuss how you're tracking before you finish your first glass of wine, or between when you order your meal and when it arrives at the table.

I don't like Fridays. Can we make it another day?

Fine, have your meeting on a different day and call it "FinFit Tuesday" (or whatever day you decide to do it). Just make sure you do it.

Find a "Best Financial Friend", your BFF!

Don't underestimate the encouragement and knowledge you can gain from a BFF. You want to find someone who's done what you are trying to do.

They've achieved what you want to achieve. They can tell you what to do and what it feels like to succeed.

They also know the mistakes you can make (because they've made them along the way), and they will tell you how to avoid them.

You see this all the time in professional sports. You've got the "old head" on the team who has been at the top of their game for a long time, who has won premierships and is generally a legend in their game. What does the coach do when a young player makes the team? They buddy him up with the old head. The best chance the young player has of being the next sporting legend is learning from the current one.

Whether you're a couple or you're single, the idea here is to include your BFF in your discussions. Don't suffer from the "I can work it myself" syndrome. Every successful athlete has a coach taking the journey with them.

It's also important to know what your BFF is *not*.

Your BFF is *not* someone who will talk you out of what you want to do and find excuses as to why you shouldn't do it.

A BFF will encourage you, give you ideas, and tell you what has worked for them and what hasn't. You want to learn from their wins and from their mistakes.

We say this with all due respect, but the truth is that family and friends generally make terrible BFFs. Remember: unless they've achieved what you want to achieve, don't ask them for help.

If you're a couple, then your BFF will be your partner, but don't be afraid to find someone else who can be an independent pair of *ears and eyes* to guide you.

Your BFF could be anyone of the following:

- A friend
- A work colleague
- A family member (refer to our earlier point)
- An accountant
- A financial adviser
- Anyone whom you think has the credentials to help you out

So, you've got your checkpoints for success set up.

Now it's time for you to take control of your financial life!

CHAPTER 4

Take Control of Your Financial Life

Goals are the fuel for your success.

When a triathlete is standing on the edge of the water ready for their swim leg, they have a race plan before they even jump into the water.

They know what split times they want to try and complete for each leg of the race, when they should consume liquid and eat food along the race course, and what other competitors they need to be in front of at each leg of the race.

The strategy is set up front so they will maximise their chance of crossing the line first.

They have set goals for the race.

As you start your journey to financial fitness, it's important to have goals.

We love goals!

Goal Setting

You turn dreams into reality by having goals.

Goal setting is a powerful process for thinking about your ideal future, and for motivating yourself to turn your vision of this future into reality. The process of setting goals helps you choose where you want to go in your life.

We have taught our boys about goals from a very young age. We have shared the importance of setting a goal, and we love seeing their sense of achievement when they achieve their goals.

Our son, Rhys, has had a passion for cars from a very young age. It was no surprise to us when he told us he wanted to apply for a job when he was old enough to work so he could save money to pay cash for his first car.

He did the research on how you get a job at McDonalds, put together his own resume, and applied online. He was successful in the interview, and his first job was at McDonalds in Fortitude Valley.

He then opened an online savings account with Westpac that gave him bonus interest if he made at least one deposit per month and no withdrawals. This account was separate from his everyday account and he used it to save for his car.

He would take every shift possible at McDonalds. He worked after school, on the weekends, during the school holidays, and even did overnight shifts to get a higher hourly rate. We remember trying to arrange a family holiday during the year that Rhys was saving for his car, but he didn't want to go because he preferred to make money and get closer to achieving his goal. We supported him every step of the way and we did not go on any family getaways that year so he could save enough money.

He also spent a lot of time looking at cars online and he worked out what he wanted—either a Toyota 86 or a Subaru BRZ.

Rhys turned 16 on January 12th and passed his learner's test on the same day. On the 26th August of that same year, he had saved enough to pay cash for his red Toyota 86. He then passed his Provisional Licence on the day of his 17th birthday. He wanted to get his car *before* he got his full licence, so he could practice driving a manual car and make sure he passed the test, *the first time*, in his own car rather than using the driving school's car.

We were so proud walking into the car dealership with Rhys to watch him pay cash for his very first car.

He set a goal, he had extreme focus, and he did not let anything get in the way of him achieving his goal.

He did, however, have to make sacrifices in order to achieve his goal.

He was working weekends to earn double time while all his mates were socialising.

You're not going to hit your target if you don't have something to aim at!

The target is important but aiming for it is just as important.

Your "aim" is your "focus."

Rhys had his target—it was his Toyota 86. And his aim was saving enough money to get it.

Want to find out how to set your target?

Let's create some **C.O.R.E. goals**.

When you are training in the gym, it is important to focus on your *core*. Your core is your abs. Core exercises will improve your balance and stability and give you that six-pack you have always wanted!

We have used the acronym **C.O.R.E.** for our goal setting because goals are the core of your financial fitness journey.

C.O.R.E. stands for:

> **C**reate – Define your goal or goals.
>
> **O**bsess – You want to live and breathe your goals. They should be so important to you that you would be shattered if you didn't achieve them.
>
> **R**esource – What do you need to achieve your goals?
>
> **E**valuate – Are you on track to achieve your goals?

Exceptional athletes are extremely good at doing this. They want to succeed, they've defined what success looks like, and they live and breathe it every day. They set up their environment around them so it's focused on achieving their goal. They are checking their progress daily, weekly, monthly to make sure they are on track.

Do you think the eight gold medals Usain Bolt won at Olympic track competitions were "nice to haves" for him and that he felt "really lucky to have won?"

No.

He knew what he wanted to achieve, and he didn't stop until he had achieved it.

His training consisted of:

- Ninety minutes in the gym every day, doing workouts that were geared toward improving his speed and agility while maintaining an athletic body.
- Speed training on the track, where he concentrated on the phases within a sprint race, which are: 1) the Starting Blocks, 2) Acceleration, and 3) Top End Speed.
- A strict diet plan, which was tough for him because he loves chicken wings and chicken nuggets.

He surrounded himself with the right people to help him make sure he achieved his goal.

He tracked his progress at pre-set intervals to make sure he was on track to achieve the goal.

His training regime and attitude were all focused on winning his races.

You can do the same with your goals. Use **C.O.R.E.**: Create, Obsess, Resource, Evaluate.

- *CREATE your goal.*

Simple really. What is it that you want to achieve?

Write your goal down. The format should be something like:

"I want to achieve XYZ by this date/time frame. "

Rhys' goal was: "I want to buy a Toyota 86, with cash, two months before my 17th birthday."

- *OBSESS over your goal.*

You should be so obsessed with achieving your goal to the point where there will be tears if you don't achieve it.

It's a "must have!" If you're not going to be disappointed if you don't achieve your goal, then it's not a goal. It was just a "nice to have." Ah well, better luck next time.

Visualise your goal. Put pictures of what it looks like *everywhere* to remind you.

Rhys was searching the internet, regularly, to find his car. He researched the year, model, and colour he wanted. He looked at the accessories he wanted and, importantly to him, what he didn't want.

By the time he was close to achieving his goal, he knew exactly what his car looked like.

He would drive us crazy, continually showing us cars, and wanting to look at car yards every weekend.

Do you see the obsession?

- *RESOURCE your goal.*

Typically, goals require money, and you also need time to achieve them.

You need to save money for your goal. The money isn't going to just appear when you need it.

Rhys knew how much he needed to save to buy his Toyota 86. He also knew he needed a job to earn the money, so he went out and got one.

- *EVALUATE how you are tracking to achieve your goal.*

Goals aren't set and then forgotten. You need to keep an eye on how you're tracking.

What system are you going to use to determine if you are on track to achieve your goal?

Rhys checked his bank account regularly. He knew how much he needed in his account at the end of every week in order to make sure he was on target to achieve his saving goal.

There could be "speed bumps" along the way that impact your plan, so you may need to adjust what you are doing to get back on track—but make sure you get back on track asap.

If Rhys had a week where he wasn't able to save the required amount, he would re-evaluate and then try and increase his savings for the following weeks so he could get back on track.

If he hadn't been consistently evaluating his progress along the way, he wouldn't have been able to adapt and make the necessary changes so he could still achieve his goal.

What if that "speed bump" turns out to be a "brick wall" and you can't achieve your goal?

It happens; life is not linear. If this happens, don't despair; just re-evaluate and re-adjust your goal. You might need more money or more time to achieve it. That's if your goal is still important to you, of course!

What if you need help achieving your goal?

Just like a sports coach can help with technique, tactics, and strength and agility training, a financial coach can help you with ideas, financial structuring, legislation, and importantly, encouragement!

It's also important that your financial coach has the formal accreditation to deliver the advice you are looking for. And it's even more important that they have achieved the financial fitness goals *you* are trying to achieve. This way you know that *they* are "practicing" what they are "preaching." You want to be confident that they can give you the right guidance.

You also want to avoid negative people. If your goal is important to you, the last thing you need is a "naysayer" trying to derail your efforts. Find people who have similar dreams and aspirations. You can use their energy to help you along the way.

"Let negative people be lonely!!!" we say.

Celebrate your success… we love a reward!

Nothing feels better than achieving. You put the effort in and you smashed your goal!

You feel extra good about yourself! Celebrate your success! Celebrate it with friends or family.

In fact, make it part of the process. It will give you that extra motivation to succeed if there is an additional reward at the end.

Rhys definitely celebrated! He put 700 kilometres on the car in the first week. He showed all his friends. He had the biggest grin on his face!

Goals like buying your first car, buying your own home, paying off your credit card debt that you've had for a long time, buying your first investment property, or reaching financial independence should be celebrated! They are big achievements!

You can include your family and friends, or maybe one best friend, or a partner, but *celebrate* your success!

When you accomplish something and don't take the time to celebrate, you rob yourself of an important feeling, an important body experience that *reinforces* your success.

How many goals should you have?

You only have so much time and energy to dedicate to each goal.

If you have too many goals, you'll spread your time and energy out too thinly, and you won't achieve any of them.

You should have no more than five goals on your plate at any one time.

Go for "quality" not "quantity," and you'll succeed.

We have the following goals:

1. Fund our son Rocco's school education without going into debt.
2. Go on a family holiday every year.
3. Pay off our home loan within the next 10 years.
4. Put ourselves in a financial position where we can choose to *retire* when we turn 60.

Once you've achieved one of your goals, look at adding another one—after you celebrate your achievement of course!

You've set yourself up for success, so what next?

You've now given yourself a purpose. You have a target you can aim at.

Focus on your **C.O.R.E goals** and you will have the foundation to get you to financial fitness.

Remember, your **C.O.R.E goals** are:

C – **C**reate

O – **O**bsess

R – **R**esource

E – **E**valuate

You've set your goals! Well done!

Before you get to work, figure out where you're starting from.

Remember that health check you completed? Well, now's the time to improve your problem areas.

What things in your financial situation could hinder you or even stop you from achieving success?

Let's start by improving your financial *diet*.

CHAPTER 5

Is your financial diet on point or are you on your way to a financial heart attack?

You'll be financially healthier if you don't spend money on the things you don't need.

Don't be lured by those items on sale. The retailers need to move their stock quickly because they don't want things sitting on the shelves for too long. They need to generate cash flow quickly to make sure they can pay their bills, pay their staff, and generate a profit for their shareholders.

They want you to think you are getting a bargain!

If you don't need it, don't buy it!

Look at ways to *save* money, not spend it.

This is the most fundamental part of your journey to financial fitness.

Don't get us wrong though; you still need to have a little fun in life. If you remove all your spending on coffees, lunches with friends, special occasions, and the occasional nice piece of clothing, you're going to be living a boring life.

If you want to have fun and a happy life, plan for it, and allocate money for it.

Just make sure you have money that you can allocate to achieving your important goal or goals.

At the end of this chapter, you should have in place:

- Extra money left over at the end of each month
- A banking structure to help you save money
- A monitoring system so you can track what you've spent your money on

What's Your Spending Plan?

What do you spend money on?

It's a reasonable question, and one that many people can't answer.

You need to know what you're spending your money on so you can see if you need to make changes.

Every elite athlete knows that what they eat can impact their performance.

Great eating choices = excellent performance
Bad eating choices = poor performance

The same can be said for your financial fitness.

Great spending choices = excellent financial performance
Bad spending choices = poor financial performance

We want you to complete a budget. We know that most people hate the word "budget" and that they find it extremely difficult to stick to one.

To move away from the stigma associated with the word "budget," let's now refer to it as your "spending plan."

You need to know what you are spending your hard-earned money on.

A **budget template** (oops, make that spending plan template) is an effective way of documenting this. If you type "budget planner" into Google, you'll find hundreds of options.

We promise we won't use the word *budget* from now on.

One quick and easy method is to use a spreadsheet program like Microsoft Excel. Go to FinFit.com.au/resources for a copy of the Excel template that we use.

If you're not good with a computer, then pen, paper, and a calculator will work just fine.

What you want to see when you complete your spending plan is where your money is coming from (i.e., your income) and where your money is going (i.e., your expenses).

Look at your bank statements and credit card statements to complete this exercise. Remember that this is a look at what you spend your money on, so write down the actual figures.

This is an extremely important part of getting financially fit. Once you've *admitted* to your spending habits, you can find ways to make better choices.

You need a spending plan in place to achieve financial fitness.

Your spending plan gives you *permission* to spend money.

However, once you've spent your allocation for an expense item, you cannot spend any more on that item until the next spending cycle.

To explain this with an example, if you have allocated $60 a week to buying lunches in your spending plan, then once you've reached your $60 for the week you cannot buy any more lunches until the following week.

We often get asked about what timeframe you should use for your spending plan. The easiest way is to match it up with your pay cycle. If you get paid fortnightly, then run your spending plan fortnightly. If you get paid monthly, then run your spending plan monthly.

Reduce the Junk Spending from Your Financial Diet and Set Your Spending Plan

So now you know what you spend your money on.

And it's probably clear that you spend money on nonessentials. We call this "junk spending."

Now your poor spending choices are there right in front of you.

If you want to boost your savings, reduce the junk spending in your financial diet.

Your spending is basically split up into two types of expenses:

1. The things you need to spend money on – the essential stuff. These include things like rent, home loan repayments, car payments, council rates, utility bills, and basic groceries.
2. The things you didn't need to spend money on – the non-essential stuff. These include things like eating out, coffees, extra clothing, and impulse purchases.

Let's do a short exercise here. You'll need a green highlighter and a red highlighter.

Print out *the last three months of statements* for your credit card and bank accounts.

Go through each statement, and for each item you *had* to spend money on, highlight it in *green;* and then for each item you *didn't* have to spend money on, highlight it in *red*.

How much red highlighter is all over those pages? These expenditures could have been your extra savings for the month!

Of course, what one person considers a "didn't have to spend it" might be a "had to spend it" for the next person. We're not here to tell you how to spend your money, but what we will say is that every dollar you spend has a consequence, either a "good consequence" or a "bad consequence" regarding your financial plans.

The more you spend on "good consequences" as opposed to "bad consequences," the better chance you'll have of achieving financial fitness. You need to work out where you want to spend that dollar.

Here are some easy ideas to reduce the "didn't have to spend it" items:

- Your gym membership is a classic example. If you're not going three times a week, cancel your membership. You can replace this with going on walks or runs around your neighbourhood. Some parks even have an outdoor gym.
- Cut out the impulse buying. If you need something, then plan for the expense. Don't just buy it because it looks nice and it happens to be on sale.
- Don't just go to the supermarket and fill your trolley. Sit down and plan your food for the week. Write down what you will eat for breakfast, lunch, and dinner. Put a list together to take to the supermarket and don't sway from the list. Don't be tempted by things at the end of each aisle or things you don't need!
- Instead of going to a restaurant for dinner with your friends, have your get-togethers at someone's place. You can take turns. People can bring their own drinks, and everyone can bring a course or a food item. This is better than spending $150 on dinner and drinks.

By now you've probably guessed that if you reduce the junk spending from your diet, you have the basis for your spending plan.

Reducing the junk spending from your spending plan will help ensure you have money left over each month. With that extra money, you can then make decisions as to what to do with it to help you achieve financial fitness.

Now you need to create your financial gym.

Your Financial Gym

If you have a structure, you can review how you're doing. It will stop you from overspending. It will make you think twice about each purchase.

When you look around your gym, you see plenty of weights and general fitness equipment. Typically, you will have a few go-to machines that help you to maintain your fitness.

You should treat your bank accounts like your financial fitness gym. Each account that you have has a specific purpose, and together they will get you, and keep you, financially fit.

TREADMILL

Your "Treadmill" account is your everyday account; it's what gives you the funds to maintain your daily lifestyle expenses. This one is for your expenses that occur regularly during the month. These expenses include paying your rent or your home loan repayments, your groceries, and any other regular, essential expenses that you have.

CYCLE

Your "Cycle" account is the account you use for your quarterly or annual bills. You might be thinking: "How is this account different from my Treadmill account?" These expenses come on a regular *cycle* rather than monthly or everyday expenses. Basically, these are any expenses you pay that are not levied monthly. These expenses include your utility bills, council rates, vehicle registration and insurance, and gifts on special occasions such as birthdays and

Christmas. The reason we suggest you separate these out from your Treadmill account is that you don't want to accidentally spend the money you've set aside for your bills. This might happen if you pay for these expenses from your Treadmill account.

HIGH FIVE

Your "High Five" account is the account you use for having fun. You'll deposit money in here for things like coffees, lunches, dinners, entertainment, and buying that new piece of clothing. These are things you shouldn't treat as everyday expenses but more like having a bit of fun. Everyone loves to have fun!!! HIGH FIVE!!!!

EMERGENCY

It's a good strategy to put some money away for emergencies. This is for unforeseen expenses. It could be for medical bills, car repairs, or funds you need if you've lost your job and you're looking for a new one. Most people don't consider having money for these purposes. The problem is that if an emergency comes up, you'll need to dip into your savings or, worse, go for your credit card or a personal loan to get you out of trouble. There's no hard and fast amount you need to have in this account. As a start, we suggest that you save at least three months' worth of your after-tax income in this account. If you're happy with a smaller or larger amount, that's up to you.

FINFIT

You will use your "FinFit" account to improve your financial fitness. Whatever surplus you have after allocating to your other accounts goes into this account. This is your ***most important account***.

To summarise, here are your accounts:

FinFit Financial Gym

Treadmill Account

Emergency Account

Money/Salary

Cycle Account

High Five Account

FinFit Account

You now need to start filling up these accounts.

Go back to your spending plan because you are going to go through each expense you've noted and allocate each of them to either the "Treadmill," "Cycle," or "High Five" accounts.

Any surplus you have in your spending plan will go into your "Emergency" account until you get to three months of your after-tax income. Once you reach this amount, start allocating your surplus to your "FinFit" account.

We'll show you an example of how this works a little later in this chapter.

Automate the transfers.

What you don't want to do is manually transfer funds into these accounts every time you get paid.

It's a waste of time and you could get it wrong.

Ask your employer to do a direct transfer to each of your accounts. If they can't do that, or won't do that, then have your pay go into your Treadmill account and then set up automated transfers from this account to your other accounts.

What if I want to have more bank accounts?

Go for it.

What we've given you is a basic account setup.

If you have a structure around what you are doing, then you can have as many accounts as you want. Just make sure you don't set up so many accounts that you can't keep track of them. Give them "names" on your internet banking account so you can tell what each of the accounts is for.

You might decide to have:

1.   An account for each of your kids
2.   An account dedicated to saving for a house deposit
3.   An account dedicated to paying off your credit card debt
4.   An account dedicated to saving for a holiday
5.   An account to save for Christmas time

You could have an account dedicated to each goal you want to achieve.

What bank should I use?

Good question.

They're basically all the same.

Your focus should be on what fees you are paying with your current bank.

If you are getting charged fees from your current bank for going about your day-to-day banking, then we suggest you find a bank that doesn't charge you any fees.

They are out there.

If you Google "high interest savings accounts," you'll get a get big list of options.

Second tier banks like ME Bank, Rabobank, or ING tend to offer higher interest rates than the majors.

Make sure you read the terms and conditions of the accounts because some need a minimum balance, or even a minimum regular deposit going into the account, in order to provide you with a bonus interest rate.

You can also consider using different banks for your accounts.

You may decide to use one bank for your Treadmill account where you can link a debit card to it and get funds out of an ATM when you need it, and then use another bank for your Emergency account, one that has only online access to the account and no access via an ATM. This will help to eliminate the temptation to dip into your Emergency account because it's a little harder to get to.

If you have a home loan, set up these accounts as offset accounts. Check with your bank, however, as some will let you have only one offset account. We'll explain more about offset accounts later in the book.

Tracking your performance

So how do you know if you are succeeding?

You need to set up a system where you can track how you're performing against your spending plan.

If you track your expenses regularly, you'll be able to catch areas where you might be about to overspend **before** it happens.

That's right, **before** it happens!

Have you tried stopping something **after** it's happened? Typically, you can't.

Five minutes a day is all you need…

That's how often you should be tracking your expenses against your spending plan. It's a lot easier to find five minutes a day than two hours—because two hours is probably how long it would take if you left it until the end of the month.

You've got a few options regarding what you can use to help you track your money against your spending plan:

1. Good old pen and paper – Wouldn't be our first option, but if you're not good with technology then get yourself a notebook.

2. Spreadsheet – Microsoft Excel or Google Sheets. Take your pick. It still requires you to manually enter your expenses, but you'll be able to keep it a lot neater and tidier than scrawling figures in a notebook. Using the in-built formulas will help you add up things quickly.

3. Personal Financial App – Our preferred option. There are lots of them. Type "personal financial app" into Google and you'll see what we mean. Have a look at "Pocketbook" or "MoneyBrilliant," and check out the reviews on them. You can set up a direct feed with your bank account, and your app will periodically retrieve your expenses from your bank account and categorise them for you. They do most of the work; you just need to double check that they've done it properly. Make sure you check what specific functions you want and be aware that you may have to pay for some of them as the free version of some of these apps may not give you what you're looking for. You could pay anywhere between $10 to $45 month for the "bells and whistles" version.

4. The FinFit Wealth Portal. This is available for you at finfit. com.au/resources. You'll love this one as:

    •   You will be able track all your income and expenses against your spending plan.
    •   You will have all your assets and liabilities in the one place with all the current information live fed from your bank.
    •   You can set goals and have it send you regular updates to tell you if you are on track to achieving them.

A strange thing happens when you're tracking your expenses. Before you pull out your debit card, credit card, or hard-earned cash, you will ask yourself:

> *"Do I really need to spend this amount of money on the item I'm about to buy?"*

We get this feedback a lot from our clients, and we recognise that our clients have just had a "light bulb" moment. A moment of sudden realization, enlightenment, or inspiration! Most of the time they walk away without buying the item.

CASE STUDY:
JOHN NEEDS A SPENDING PLAN

John is struggling to save money; he's spending every dollar that he earns.

He works hard for his money and he receives $5,500 a month in after-tax income. He wants to start saving *some* of it rather than spending *all* of it. Typically, he doesn't have much left of his $5,500 by the end of the month.

After analysing his bank account and credit card transactions, he was shocked at the amount of money he was spending on "shouldn't have spent it" expenses. He's decided that he is going to put some structure around his spending; that is, he's setting up a spending plan and he's going to stick to it.

JOHN'S SPENDING PLAN

John's spending plan looks like this:

1. $3,400 per month for his everyday expenses, which include rent, groceries, mobile phone, internet, fares, fuel, gym membership, haircuts, and Netflix. Also included is $400 per month for his car loan.
2. $250 per month for his bills that don't come on a monthly cycle, such as utilities, car registration, and car insurance.

3. $850 per month on fun stuff like coffees, lunches and dinners out with friends, and the odd piece of new clothing he wants to buy.
4. $1,000 per month to his savings account, which is what he has left over after all the above expenses.

He feels comfortable with an emergency fund where he has one month of his after-tax income in case he ever needs it.

HERE'S HOW JOHN TRANSFERS HIS MONEY

He creates the following account structure to help him with his spending plan:

Treadmill account – His employer won't split his income into four payments, so he will have his $5,500 per month go into this account.

Cycle account – He sets up an automated transfer of $250 per month from his Treadmill account to this account to occur a day after he gets paid. This is for his quarterly and annual bills.

High Five account – He sets up an automated transfer of $850 per month from his Treadmill account to this account to occur a day after he gets paid. This is for his fun stuff.

Emergency account – He sets up an automated transfer of $1,000 per month from his Treadmill account to this account to occur a day after he gets paid. This is his Emergency savings account.

FinFit account – He sets up this account but doesn't allocate any funds to it initially. Once he gets his Emergency account to $5,500, he'll then start transferring the $1,000 per month into this account.

The $3,400 he has left stays in his Treadmill account, which he'll use to manage his day-to-day expenses.

HERE'S HOW HE KEEPS TRACK OF HIS SPENDING

John wants to make it simple for himself to track and monitor how he is doing. So, he downloaded a personal finance app onto his smartphone and linked all his accounts to it. He can now see how much he has in each account. He can also set limits on each of his accounts, so he can see how much he is withdrawing from each account to fund his expenses compared to what he set up initially as his spending plan.

He has now set up the foundation he needs to get financially fit. He has a structure in place where he has every confidence he can achieve his financial goals.

Why is it important to have a spending plan?

Your spending plan will tell you where your funds should go.

Your financial gym will make sure the funds are there, in the right place, when you need them.

You track your progress so that if you need to make any changes, you can do it *before* it becomes a problem.

Remove the financial stress from your life.

Think of the bigger picture here. Cash is king, right?

How much can you realistically achieve if you don't have the money available when you need it?

Many of the things you want to do in your life require you to have the money to do them, such as putting a roof over your head, putting food on the table, having fun, putting your kids through school, and planning for your future. All these need $$$$.

The amount of financial stress you'll have in life is directly related to how much surplus money you have in the bank.

We all know that stress isn't good for us.

According to the "Survey of attitudes towards the Australian health system" carried out by the Menzies Centre for Health Policy at the University of Sydney, families under financial stress are more likely to suffer poorer health.

No surplus money in the bank account
= High Stress Levels

Some surplus money in the bank account
= Medium Stress Levels

Lots of surplus money in the bank account
= Low Stress Levels

Having a structure around how you manage money and directing it to the right places will get you financially fit!

Take your spending plan to the next level

A good coach will research their team's next opponent. What are the team's strengths? What are the team's weaknesses? What is the best way to beat them? The coach won't just send the team out without a game plan.

Look at how you're funding your expenses so you can work out if there is a more efficient way to manage them.

Look for extra savings…keep your money in your pocket rather than someone else's!

When was the last time one of your service providers rang you up and said, "Hey, you know what, you've been a great customer for such a long time, so we are going to give you a discount on your bill!"

What!? Never!

There is a reason for that.

When you're apathetic regarding your bills, the more money they make and the less money you save.

You've got so much scope to save money with this one.

Look at everything that you're spending money on and work out if you can get it cheaper.

This will require you to ring your providers and ask for a discount.

A LITTLE RESEARCH FOR THOSE DISCOUNTS

Before you do that, you need to do your research. For this, Google is your best friend.

Look at other service providers to see what they charge. You might get that information from a website or you may have to call them. Also, there are comparison websites that can do some of the leg work for you.

If you come across a provider that looks to be cheaper than your current one, note down the details of their deal.

Your current service provider is more likely to give you a better deal if they can see you've done your research and you are serious about leaving. Just ringing them up and asking for a discount is unlikely to work.

You could say something like:

"Hi, I've been looking around at other providers and I see that I can get a lower cost for the same service with *XYZ*. What's the best price you can give me for your service, so I can compare your offer to their offer?"

It's important to sound confident over the phone. If you're fumbling through the call, then the person on the other end of the phone won't take you seriously.

Now, the response they give you could go one of two ways:

1. "Yes, Mrs. Smith, you've been such a great customer and we are happy to give you a discount."
2. "Thanks for your offer, Mrs. Smith, but you already have the best price we can offer."

Most providers will look at giving you a discount. It's easier and cheaper for them to retain an existing customer than to try and find a new customer.

The second they think you are going to take your business elsewhere, they will be more accommodating with your request.

This will work with:

- Utility providers (water, gas, electricity)
- Internet providers
- Mobile phone providers
- Health insurance providers

- Home and Contents insurance
- Car insurance
- Just about any provider really

The 15 minutes you spend on the phone with each of your providers can save you hundreds of dollars.

Even if they do give you a discount, it doesn't mean it's the lowest cost service. Keep shopping around for a better deal.

We recently renegotiated our private health insurance with our provider. What prompted this was a letter we received from them that indicated our monthly premium was going to increase by $47 per month.

So, we called our provider. After discussing what we were covered for, we decided that we could increase the excess on our hospital coverage, and go for an extras cover that didn't need things like hip replacement and pregnancy cover. We figured that we were a little young for needing a hip replacement and we certainly weren't needing coverage for pregnancy related services anymore!

This 15-minute discussion saved us $193 a month on our insurance premium!

There's another $193 a month going into our FinFit account!

Never pay full price for anything!

We both swear by this one.

If we do need to get something that doesn't fit into the "Had to spend it" expenses bucket, we wait for it to come on sale. We wait for a deal. We look at discount sites like "Scoupon" or "Groupon" where you can get some significant discounts.

If we spot something in a shop we want to buy, we wait until it goes on sale.

We don't buy because it's on sale. We buy it because we need it and then we wait until it goes on sale before we do buy it.

Spring clean your house and make money.

Time to make some money from all those unwanted or unused items you have.

Let's start with your wardrobe. Are there any clothes, bags, or shoes that you can sell?

Have a look at the whole family's wardrobe and see if there are items that have not been used for over 12 months.

After you finish with your wardrobe, look at the rest of your house for items you no longer use that someone else would use.

You may have books, jewellery, furniture, computers, artwork, sporting goods, and so much more!

If you have children, this is also the perfect time to look at toys they no longer use.

There is no point hanging onto these items if you're not going to use them. You might as well make some money on them and deposit the money into your FinFit account. Just make sure whatever you intend to sell is in decent condition, so someone will buy it.

There are plenty of options available to you to sell them:

1. eBay or Gumtree – Probably two of the most well-known of all online sales websites, these are great ways to earn some extra dollars. Create an account and you can start selling

straight away! All payments are made through PayPal, making for safe and easy transactions.

2. Facebook pages – There are so many Facebook pages that you can use to sell items. Check out your local area for "buy, sell, and swap" sites. Some are public and some are private. It is super easy to find them and then advertise your goods.

3. Local markets – Check out some local markets and take everything there for the day.

4. Garage sales – You would be amazed at what people will buy at a garage sale.

You're managing your spending plan like a champion, so what's next?

What you choose to spend your money on will directly impact how quickly you get to financial fitness. It will also determine how long you will *stay* financially fit.

Remember, if you don't *need* to buy it, walk away!

After reading this chapter:

- You've looked at what you've been spending money on and identified all the junk spending you've been doing.
- You've taken proactive steps to reduce the junk spending from your financial diet and you've committed to make good spending decisions.
- You now have more surplus money left over each month.
- Your financial gym gives you the edge you need to make sure you're going to achieve financial fitness. You'll have money when you need it.

- You've got a system in place to track what you're spending your money on.

Let's now look at that financial flab you've cultivated over the years and how we might make you lean and mean.

CHAPTER 6

Are you lean or are you carrying extra financial weight?

The bad debt you have is that financial flab that is weighing you down.

Your financial flab is your debt. Specifically, bad debt.

That includes credit cards, personal loans, and car loans.

You want to get rid of your bad debt as quickly as possible. You can then allocate the money you were using to pay off your bad debt to improving your financial fitness.

At the end of this chapter you'll have:

- An understanding of the difference between bad debt and good debt.
- A strategy in place to repay your debt quicker.
- A monitoring system so you can track your debt reduction.

Why do we get debt flabby?

As humans, we can't help ourselves.

We like instant gratification, and the less we have to work for it, the better it makes us feel. But that instant gratification can be followed by a long period of regret.

Why save for that $5,000 holiday when I can borrow the money **now** and pay it back **later**?

Why train for that 10K road run when I can turn up on race day and just run it? Surely running 10K is not that hard?

A great athlete will build up to that race. They'll know the date of the race and they'll develop their training plan. When the starting gun goes off, they will be at their peak physical and mental fitness.

If they haven't trained for the race, it's highly unlikely that they will win, and they may not even finish. And they'll probably feel terrible, physically and mentally.

Training is just like saving for that brand new television you want. You know the date you want it, and you've saved on a regular basis so when you walk into the store, you'll pay cash for it.

Not training is like borrowing the money you need for the television. You turn up at the store with your credit card. Then you have to deal with repaying the cost of the television as well as paying interest payments.

The reward for training (i.e., saving) is not having to deal with the physical and mental pain after the race (i.e., the interest payments).

Good Fat, Bad Fat—Good Debt, Bad Debt

This isn't going to be a science lecture on which are good fats and which are bad fats, and we are certainly not experts in this field. Most people are aware that there are good fats out there that you should try and consume. Fats contained in vegetable oils, Omega-3 fats found in some fish, and the fats found in nuts are the good guys. Fats contained in animal fat are the bad guys.

The same can be said about debt.

Good debt is basically any debt you have that has helped you acquire an asset that is going to help you achieve financial fitness. That asset is used to create wealth for you over the long term.

Examples of wealth-creating assets are shares and investment properties. They are assets that will grow in value, and that may provide you with some income along the way, through dividends and rent. We'll discuss more about these later.

Bad debt is basically any debt you've used to buy the "wants" in your life. The stuff that gives you short-term gratification but long-term pain. Remember the example we used on the previous page about buying your brand-new television with your credit card. That's an example of bad debt.

The more bad debt you have, the more financially unfit you are. Why? Because every dollar you're spending on repaying that debt is a dollar that you could be using to make a better financial future for yourself.

The typical attributes of bad debt are:

- You're using debt to buy something that is going to decline in value, like a car or a boat.
- You don't receive any income from the item you've bought.
- You can't claim a tax deduction on the interest on your loan.

The typical attributes of good debt are:

- You're using debt to buy something that is going to increase in value, like a house.
- You receive income from the item you've bought, such as rent.
- You can claim a tax deduction on the interest on the loan.

Which type of debt would you like to have?

The bad debt you have is that financial flab that is weighing you down. It's diverting your hard-earned money into something that isn't going to improve your financial fitness.

Okay, I've got financial flab. How do I get rid of it?

You got yourself into this situation because you couldn't help yourself.

If you burn more calories than you consume, you lose weight.

If you pay more than the minimum amount off your debt, you'll pay it off quicker and you'll pay a lot less interest than if you go to the full loan term.

Remember the financial gym we introduced you to in Chapter 5?

Your FinFit account is your go-to account. It's your decision on how much of your monthly surplus you are going to use to go towards paying extra on your debt.

Let's look at an example. If you have a $25,000 car loan with an interest rate of 8.5 percent and a loan term of five years, the monthly repayment would be $513. Let's just say you've got $500 per month going into your FinFit account each month. You decide to allocate an extra $250 per month to repaying your debt, and to reduce the amount going into your FinFit account to $250 per month. You will make an extra $250 per month repayment onto your car loan, which takes your repayment to $763 per month.

By making that decision, your car loan will be paid off one year and 10 months earlier and you will save $2,227.57 in interest payments.

You've reduced your loan term by 37 percent and reduced the amount of interest you've paid by a whopping 61 percent!

As you can you see, if you have surplus funds each month and you have the bank account structure in place, you can repay your debt faster.

Once you pay your debt off, you've freed up more money, which will go into your FinFit account. You can then use it to improve your financial fitness even more.

Using our car loan example, that's an extra $513 per month going into your FinFit account!

I'll just use my credit card

Ah yes, the credit card. "Credit" is a word that makes people feel good about themselves. When you take credit for something, it usually means you've done something fantastic and you'll take the accolades for it.

But your credit card is not a "credit" card. The only one taking credit for it is the financial institution that gave it to you in the first place. Of course, they want you to use credit so they will receive all that lovely interest you'll be paying them.

The banks want you to pay interest—that's how they make their money. But instead, how about you keep the interest *yourself* and use it to help *you* become financially fit...

Hot tip on your credit card: DON'T USE IT LIKE A CREDIT CARD!!!

Sorry for yelling.

Treat your credit card as "plastic cash." Remember that spending plan you did? Well, your credit card is a *tool* you use to help you pay for stuff in your spending plan. It's convenient. But it's *your* money you're spending.

What do we mean by "your money?"

We'll give you an example.

Let's assume that your spending plan says you're going to spend $100 a week for lunches during the work week. You walk into the café, order your food, wave your credit card over the card reader, and walk away with your order when it's ready.

When your credit card bill is due, you pay the $100. Not $60 or $70, but $100.

Why? Because you noted in your spending plan that you're spending $100 a week on lunch. Not $70 plus the interest I'm going to pay on my credit card when I don't pay the full amount.

You stick to your spending plan, you use your credit card to pay for things in your spending plan, then you pay your credit in full when your credit card bill is due. You pay ZERO interest!

Think of the interest you pay on your credit card to the bank as an *illegal performance enhancing drug*. It empowers you; it makes you feel strong and fast. YOU CAN PAY FOR ANYTHING!!!

Knock! Knock! —Mandatory Drug Test!!!

When the drug testers come knocking on your door for your sample, you're not going to come out of this well.

If you're paying an unnecessary *interest* payment, you're wasting your money!

"But I want the credit card points..."

There are lots of credit cards out there that allow you to accrue points, and you can cash in your points on just about anything.

Don't use your credit card to accrue points. Use your credit card to help you implement your spending plan. The reward you get for sticking to your spending plan is the reward points that you receive.

You can then use the points to buy yourself a little reward for sticking to your spending plan and not paying any unnecessary interest.

"But I can't help myself..."

Cut the credit card up and get yourself a *debit card*. The debit card will make sure you are only spending your own money. The debit card will link to your Treadmill account.

The reality is, the more reasons you come up with to use bad debt, the more of a drag you create on your financial fitness plan.

What about these 0 percent balance transfer credit cards to help me pay off my credit card?

This involves transferring the debt from one card to another with the new card having a lower initial interest rate for a specified time.

We recently had a client with a $10,000 credit card debt. They'd maxed out their card and the interest rate on their card was 20.99 percent.

They wanted to repay the credit card in 24 months.

We crunched the numbers and presented them with two options:

1.   Make extra repayments on their current card – To repay their credit card in 24 months, they would need to make repayments of $513.81 per month. Their total repayments over the 24 months would be $12,331.

2.   Transfer the $10,000 to a credit card offering zero interest – We found an option for them that had no transfer fee and an annual fee of $99. The interest-free period was 25 months. To pay their card off in 24 months meant that they would need to repay $424.92 per month. Their total repayments over the 24 months would be $10,198.

They chose option two because:

1.   It had a lower monthly repayment.
2.   It would save them $2,133 in repayments over the 24 months.

When you're looking at this strategy to repay your credit card, you need to consider the following:

1.   The transfer fee – This is charged as a percentage of the amount being transferred. This could be anywhere between 0 percent and 2 percent.
2.   The annual fee – This could be as high as $150 a year. Some providers waive the first year's fee but charge the fee from year two onwards.
3.   For this to really work, you should repay the card, in total, during the interest-free period.
4.   The card will revert to a predetermined interest rate after the 24 months. You should make sure this rate is lower than the rate on your old card.
5.   Anything you purchase on the new card during the initial interest-free period will not be subject to the 0 percent interest rate. You should make sure you don't use this card for purchases during the interest-free period.

This strategy can work for you, but you really need to do your research before you consider using it.

What flabby debt areas should I target first?

We introduced the concept of good debt and bad debt earlier. To refresh your memory:

Good debt – debt you've used to acquire wealth-creating assets with the aim of trying to achieve the long-term goal of financial fitness.

Bad debt – debt you've used to buy the "wants" in your life—the stuff that gives you short-term gratification but long-term pain.

Which of them should you start to repay first?

Simple. Start with the bad debt first.

You should work on the quick wins first. You want to create momentum in your debt repayment strategy, and you want to feel like you are making progress. Why? It makes you feel good when you've paid one of your debts off in full.

If something makes you feel good, then you'll keep doing it.

Kate has the following debts to her name:

1. Car Loan – amount still owing is $20,000, and the interest rate is 8 percent.
2. Credit Card – amount still owing is $10,000, and the interest rate is 20.99 percent.
3. Personal Loan – amount still owing is $2,000, and the interest rate is 11 percent.

Kate's logical thinking suggests that she should focus on repaying the debt with the highest interest rate first, as this will save her more interest than paying off one of the debts with a lower interest rate.

Her logic is correct.

However, she can see that her personal loan is almost paid off, and it has a lot lower amount owing than the car loan and the credit card.

She thinks, "Wouldn't it be great to repay that personal loan first?"

The best way to create some momentum in your debt repayment strategy is to repay the smallest debt off first, if you can do it in a really short time frame, even if the interest rate is higher than your other debt.

Once Kate has paid off her personal loan, she has two debts left and she can now focus on the next one. The credit card is next on her list.

It's your choice on which bad debt to tackle first. *You* come up with the debt repayment game plan, but if you want to see results, it's important that you stick to that plan.

What about the debt on my own home?

Wouldn't it be nice to pay off your home loan as soon as possible?

Think of your home loan as a really big personal loan. The strategy around repaying it quickly is no different than repaying a credit card or a car loan.

Here are three tips to repay your home loan faster.

Tip 1 – Lower your interest rate.

According to a recent survey by KPMG, 61 percent of Australians who were surveyed renegotiated their home loans at least once every five years.

Our response to this is:

1. 39 percent of Australians are paying way too much in interest on their home loan; and
2. Five years is way too long to leave your renegotiation.

You should be renegotiating at least every two years. It's a very competitive market out there among all the banks, and they are always trying to attract new borrowers—especially since 39 percent of these borrowers don't bother to renegotiate their loan interest!

You'd think that banks would offer the best rates to their existing customers. Unfortunately, they don't. They are more likely to offer better rates to new loan customers than to existing ones.

When was the last time your home loan provider rang you up and said, "Hey, we've got a great deal on home loans this month, and we've decided to lower your rate by 0.5 percent!"

Never? Are you surprised?

Let's play the "See how much lower I can get my home loan interest rate" game.

The first thing you need to do is find out what other banks are offering to new customers regarding home loan interest rates.

Once you've found a rate that is lower than the one you have with your bank, write down the name of the bank and the interest rate.

Next, ring your bank and ask for a payout figure for your home loan because you want to refinance with the bank you just found that has a lower interest rate.

This should trigger a transfer to the bank's retention team where they'll likely reduce your interest rate to keep you from leaving.

However, don't be surprised if they don't match the interest rate that you could get from the other bank. They'll probably get to within 0.5 percent of it.

Your bank knows how time consuming it is for you to change to another bank.

When you move to another bank, you've got to change all your direct debits and credits that you have set up on your old accounts to all your new accounts. This takes time and most people can't be bothered to do it.

Your bank makes money from your apathy.

This is where *you* are different. You will make the change, because it's going to save you thousands of dollars over the term of your loan.

If you have a $400,000 home loan on a 4.5 percent principle and interest payment, and you get a reduction in interest rate to 4 percent, then your repayments could be reduced by $117.08 per month. That equates to a $42,149 reduction in interest payments over the term of the loan, assuming a 30-year loan term.

Once you've got the interest reduction from your existing bank, you need to work out whether it's worthwhile to move to another bank anyway. If your current bank reduces your rate to 4 percent, but the other bank offers 3.5 percent, it may still be worth moving.

Don't feel as if you have any loyalty to your bank, even if you've been a customer for a very long time. If there was any loyalty in banking, you would already have the lowest rate available.

If your existing bank won't lower their rate, then it's time to switch banks!

Tip 2 – Increase the amount and frequency of your payments.

On a typical 30-year mortgage, anything extra you pay in the first five to eight years will cut your interest bill and shorten the life of your loan. This is because most of your repayments go towards paying off the interest component of the loan rather than the principle component.

The most important thing to know about home loans is that interest is calculated on the daily balance and charged to the loan account monthly in arrears.

One of the easiest ways to pay down your mortgage faster is to make your home loan repayments *fortnightly* instead of monthly.

If you get paid fortnightly, you'll find this is an easy and convenient way to make your repayments—and there's no need to pay more *money* to make a big difference.

Just by splitting your mortgage payment in two and *paying more often*, you can cut years off your loan term and save a lot of money in interest.

There are 26 fortnights in a year, but only 12 months. By paying fortnightly, you will be effectively making the same as 13 monthly repayments every year—paying more without making an impact on your spending plan.

If you have a home loan of $400,000 with an interest rate of 4 percent per year paying principle and interest repayments with a loan term of 30 years, then the monthly repayment on this loan would be approximately $1,910 per month. If you divide the $1,910 by two and pay $955 a fortnight instead, *you'd shave four years and one month off the loan term, and you'd save $45,080 in repayments!!*

Tip 3 – Attach an offset account to your home loan.

An offset account is a transaction account linked to your home loan. The money you have in this account will offset the interest you owe on your home loan; that is, you'll pay only the interest on your home loan less your offset balance.

If you have a home loan of $400,000 and you have $20,000 sitting in the offset account, then you are only paying interest on $380,000 (i.e. $400,000 – $20,000 = $380,000).

If you have a home loan of $400,000 with an interest rate of 4 percent per year paying principle and interest repayments with a loan term of 30 years, then the monthly repayment on this loan would be approximately $1,910 per month. If you have $20,000 constantly sitting in the offset account attached to this loan, then you'd shave one year and 10 months off the loan term and save $42,813 in interest!

Some banks will allow you to have multiple offset accounts. All the accounts you set up as your spending plan gym could be used to offset your home loan.

The debt flab scales are your friend!

When you're on a weight loss program, there's usually a step in the process to work out how you're tracking. Some people use scales, others look at their belt size or whether they fit back into clothes they haven't been able to wriggle into for a long time.

Whatever method you use, you want to see how you are doing. Are you succeeding?

The same goes for debt repayment. Put something in place that will help you work out how you are going to track your progress.

Keep it simple.

If you're good with spreadsheets, track your debt balances on spreadsheets, and look at them every month to see how you're doing.

If you're not good with spreadsheets, get yourself a notebook—call it the "Debt Flab Smasher" if you like, or some other name that will motivate you—and write down your debt balances each month.

The personal finance app you downloaded to help you track your spending plan may also be able to track your debt balances.

Your total bad debt balance owing should reduce each month, but at a faster rate than if you just paid the minimum amount in repayments. If it isn't reducing, you need to go back to your spending plan, and work out what you need to change.

You've got your debt flab reduction plan in place. What's next?

Use debt for *good*, not for *evil*. The *good* debt will create wealth for you and get you financially fit. The *evil* debt will create a drag on your financial fitness because every dollar you're spending on repaying that debt is a dollar that you could be using to make a better financial future for yourself.

After reading this chapter you should have:

- An understanding of the difference between bad debt and good debt.
- A strategy to repay your "bad" debt as quickly as possible.

- A system to review your debt level on a regular basis to make sure you're reducing it as planned.

Now let's have a look at what to do with the surplus money you now have each month.

CHAPTER 7

Your financial muscles – are you using them or losing them?

If you want to build muscles, you have to work them.

To do that, you might have a training plan that:

1. Has you eating the right type of food.
2. Makes you increase the weights you are lifting over time.
3. Works several muscle groups at once.

4.   Has you training on a regular basis.

Building your financial muscle needs a similar training plan:

You need to:

1.   Use the funds in your FinFit account.
2.   Try to accumulate different investment assets over time.
3.   Take the right level of investment risk.
4.   Add to your investment assets on a regular basis.

Using your financial muscle will get you to peak financial fitness.

After reading this chapter you should:

- Know what investment options you have available to you.
- Know how much investment risk you should be taking.
- Be adding to your investments on a regular basis.

What are my investment muscle-building options?

There are a lot of options.

When you look around a gym floor, you have so many choices regarding what weights and machines you can use.

If you're a beginner, you will typically go for the option that gives you a quick workout that won't cause you too much pain and discomfort.

If you're more advanced, you'll go for something that's going to push you a little harder to help you achieve your fitness goal.

You can look at your financial fitness goals in the same way.

If you're just beginning, then keep things simple.

Your investment options are:

- Cash
- Fixed Income
- Shares
- Property.

Let's tackle each one and give you a little more detail about each.

Cash

Your "FinFit" account is a type of cash investment.

These accounts generally offer lower returns compared to other investment types, but the chance of losing your money is extremely low. Note that we said "...is extremely low." However, there is a chance, although very slim, that the bank where you have your money could go bust, and you could lose your money. To avoid this situation from ever happening, the Australian Government has guaranteed deposits of up to $250,000 in Authorised Deposit-Taking Institutions.

You typically don't get a very good rate of interest in these types of accounts, so you would only use them to park money in for short periods of time. Historically, the return on cash has been tracking between 2 to 3 percent over the last 10 years and that's on high interest accounts, not on your normal everyday transaction account.

If you have a short-term goal you want to save for, this would be the type of account you'd use.

You don't get any capital growth with this type of investment. You are only receiving the interest that is being paid to you.

Investing in cash is like taking a leisurely stroll through the park or along the river. You're not going to build much in the way of muscle by doing it, but the chances of injury are very low.

Fixed Income

We're talking a little more intensity than your leisurely stroll through the park. You're taking a BodyPump class where you want to burn a few more calories and get a little leaner, toned, and fit. There's a little more chance of injury but not much. And it's not your go-to workout if you want to build big muscle.

The interest rates are typically higher than cash, as you are essentially lending your money to the issuer for an agreed term, and as compensation for that, they will pay you a fixed rate of interest over the time they borrow the money from you. You are taking a little more risk.

There is typically no capital growth component to this investment.

The ones you may have heard a lot about are "bonds." Bonds are an example of a fixed income investment. There are many examples of bonds, such as government bonds or corporate bonds.

Government bonds are issued by governments. Let's say the Australian Government needs to borrow money to fund the construction of a new train line. They might issue a 10-year bond with an interest rate of 3 percent per year so they can raise money to fund the project. So, if you invest in this bond, the government will pay you 3 percent per year for 10 years on the money you've lent to them and then pay you back the original money that you invested.

Corporate bonds are issued by businesses. Let's say BHP needs to borrow money to fund a new coal mine. They might issue a five-year bond with an interest rate of 5 percent per year so they can raise money to fund the project. So, if you invest in this bond, BHP will

pay you 5 percent per year for five years on the money you've lent to
them and then pay you back the original money you invested.

Bonds have ratings. A low-risk bond may have a rating of "AAA,"
which means that there is a low risk of you not getting back the
money that you originally invested. A high-risk bond may have a
rating of "BBB," which means there is a high risk of you not getting
back the money that you originally invested. The interest rate on
an "AAA" bond is typically lower than the interest rate on a "BBB"
bond. You would expect that; you want a higher return on the
"BBB" bond because you are taking a higher risk.

Your big muscle workouts are shares and property. This is where you
want to go to increase the intensity and work out every financial
muscle. To build muscle, you have to push heavy weights. To build
financial muscle, you have to push a higher risk investment. This is
where shares and property come into their own.

Shares

If you buy shares in a company, you effectively have an ownership
interest in the company. This means you are also entitled to any
distribution of profits from the company if they choose to distribute
any via a dividend.

You want the value of your shares to increase over the long term. The
value of your shares is driven by demand in that they are only worth
what someone is willing to pay for them. Because of this, there is a
chance that the value of your shares could fall.

There are many ways you can invest in shares.

You can buy them directly—by going through a stockbroker to buy
a share in most listed companies. If you want to buy $10,000 worth
of BHP shares, you can ask your stockbroker to buy them for you.

They will charge a brokerage fee for doing this, which could be a fixed dollar fee, or a percentage fee based on the trade amount.

You can buy them indirectly—by buying units in a managed fund or buying an exchange traded fund that invests in a portfolio of shares. The difference here is that you don't own the underlying share but you will typically have a more diversified portfolio than owning shares directly. Depending on the managed fund, you could have anywhere from 15 to 400 shares in the portfolio.

In a managed fund, your money is pooled together with other investors. An investment manager then buys and sells shares or other assets on your behalf, and you are usually paid income or "distributions" periodically. The value of your investment will rise or fall with the value of the underlying assets.

It also depends on how much you have to invest. If you have $10,000, you are better off investing in a managed fund, as there will be greater diversification in the investment. If you have $200,000, you may be better off with a direct share portfolio as the fees may be lower.

Shares are a great investment option if you have a long-term investment timeframe.

Property

You buy a house or unit with the intention of renting it out to a tenant to receive rental income.

As with shares, you are looking for the property to grow in value over the long term. Like shares, your property is only worth what someone is willing to pay for it.

Often, you will have to borrow money to fund the purchase of the property. The costs to purchase the property can be high, as you typically need to pay stamp duty to the relevant state government, and also pay a conveyancer or lawyer to help facilitate the transfer of the ownership of the property from the seller to you.

The amount of cash you need to have to begin with a property investment is a lot higher than investing in shares.

You need to be careful with property. Make sure you understand the cash flow of your investment.

Whilst you may receive rent from the tenant, the interest payments on your loan and the expenses to run the property, such as agent fees, maintenance costs, and council rates may be more than the rent you are receiving. You can claim a tax deduction for any net expenses you may incur on the property, but even after this deduction, the property may still have a negative cash flow.

If your property has a negative cash flow after tax, but has good capital growth prospects, then it may still be a good investment. You just need to make sure you have enough of a surplus cash flow to fund the running costs during the year.

As with shares, property can be a great investment option if you have a long-term investment timeframe.

The investment explanations above are simplistic in order to give you a basic understanding of your options. If you are not comfortable with making your own investment decisions, get some help from someone who knows what they are doing and is licensed to provide you with the advice you are looking for.

It's not risky if you understand what you are doing

Educate yourself.

If you don't understand something, there is a good chance you won't do it. Or worse, you'll do it and you'll get a bad result.

When you first start lifting weights at the gym, you don't load up the bar with 100 kg, and try and bench press it. There is a "high risk" that you are not going to be able to lift it, and there's a chance you could hurt yourself.

Instead, you load up the bar with a weight you know you can handle, lie down on the bench, and complete a few reps. You gradually increase the weight over time as you get stronger.

You've essentially performed a risk analysis. You said to yourself: I will start with a weight that I'm comfortable with and as I build muscle, and get stronger, I will increase the weight.

The bar is your investment vehicle. The weight you put on the bar is equivalent to how much risk you're willing to take.

It's only "risky" when you don't understand what you are doing.

How much risk are you going to take with your surplus money?

Why would you care about how much risk you should take?

Here's a quick summary of where each of the investment types we've mentioned sit on the risk scale.

Investment Type	Example	How Risky Is It?
Cash	Bank account	Low
Fixed Income	Bonds	Low to Medium Risk
Shares	Australian and International Shares	High
Property	Residential Property and Listed Property	High

An investment that has a low-risk rating means that the chances of you losing some of the original money you put into the investment are quite low.

A high-risk investment means the chances of you losing some of the original money you put into the investment are much higher.

Keep in mind that there is no *guarantee* you will get a return on your investment. Whether it is a low-risk or high-risk investment, there is still a chance you could lose some of your money.

To help determine how much risk you're willing to take, think about how long you want to put your money away before you withdraw it.

The financial goals you have may require you to take a certain level of investment risk depending on what you are trying to achieve.

Here's a rule of thumb:

How long do you want to invest your money?	How much risk should you take?
Less than 3 years	Low risk
Between 3 years and 7 years	Mix of low risk and high risk
More than 7 years	High risk

The more risk you take, the greater the chance that you will have a period of negative returns. To try and recover some of this negative return you need to stay in the investment for a longer period. That is why you need to invest for more than seven years when you invest in a high-risk investment.

Diversify to reduce the risk.

Some people might be tempted to just buy a single share rather than invest in a managed fund or Exchange Traded Fund where you can invest in a portfolio of shares.

Don't!

You're putting all your eggs in one basket. Easter is the only time you can put all your eggs in one basket!

You want to diversify!

If you have invested in one share and things go bad, then your whole portfolio will be affected. If you have 20 shares and one share goes bad, then you still have the other 19 shares. Diversifying by having more than one share in your portfolio gives you added protection in case something goes wrong. As a general rule of thumb, you should try to have 15 to 20 shares in your portfolio.

What history tells us.

Below is a chart, sourced from Vanguard, which shows how the Australian and US share markets have performed from 1 July 1988 to 30 June 2018. It shows what has happened to $10,000 if you invested it back on 1 July 1988 and reinvested any dividends.

The line which reaches higher to the top right is the US share market and other line is the Australian share market.

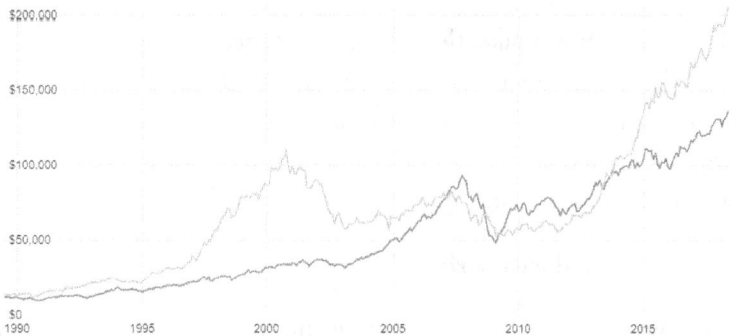

What do you notice first?

Most people focus on the "dips." The classic "sky is falling" syndrome. That is why most people don't invest. They are too scared of the "dips" and of losing their money in a market crash.

During this 30-year period we've had:

- The last Australian recession from 1990 to 1992
- Iraq invading Kuwait in 1990
- The Asian currency crisis in 1997
- The dot.com bubble bursting in 2000
- Terrorist attacks in the US in 2001
- The Bali bombings in 2002
- The second Iraq war in 2003
- The US subprime crisis in 2007 which led into the global financial crisis
- Lehman Brothers collapse in 2008
- The Gulf of Mexico oil spill in 2010
- Japanese Tsunami in 2011
- Brexit in 2016
- Australia went through five Prime Ministers from 2008 to 2017
- Trump taking office in 2017

What do we see?

If you had invested $10,000 back on 1 July 1988 in the Australian stock market and reinvested the dividends, it would have been worth $136,435 on 30 June 2018. That's an 9.1 percent per year return for 30 years! Your money would have doubled every 8 years!

If you had invested $10,000 back on 1 July 1988 in the US stock market and reinvested the dividends, it would have been worth $206,637 on 30 June 2018. That's a 10.6 percent per year return for 30 years! Your money would have doubled every seven years!

If you had invested with an equal waiting between the Australian and US stock markets, because we like to diversify, then you would have made $171,536.

There are only two important points on the chart: the day you invested your money and the day you take your money out.

What happens in between those two points is not something to be too concerned about.

As you can see from the chart, investment markets can fall. The fall can be small, or it can be large. Whether it's the share market or the property market, it can fall. Unfortunately, the people who get paid a lot of money to work out when this will happen next *rarely* work out when it will happen next.

However, investment markets also rise, and if history is any guide, they rise more times than they fall.

The tip here is to invest over the long term to reduce the impact of the "falls" and take advantage of the "rises." It is time in the market rather than timing the market.

The simplest way to start your investment journey

Sure, all this is great in theory but how do you get started?

Here's your action plan:

1. Build up the funds in your FinFit account until you get to $5,000.

    You want to keep the trading costs down so it's good to start with a reasonable amount.

2.   Open an online share trading account.

     Canstar (www.canstar.com.au) rated the following as their top online shared trading brokers:

     - Amscot
     - Bell Direct
     - CMC Markets
     - CommSec
     - nabtrade
     - Westpac

3.   Invest the $5,000 in one of Vanguard's diversified exchange traded funds depending on how much risk you're willing to take.

     Here's the list of options:

     - Vanguard Diversified Conservative ETF (ASX code VDCO)
     - Vanguard Diversified Balanced ETF (ASX code VDBA)
     - Vanguard Diversified Growth ETF (ASX code VDGR)
     - Vanguard Diversified High Growth ETF (ASX code VDHG)

4.   Watch your investment grow over the longer term

A quick word on tax.

Always remember that any income or capital gain you earn from an investment will be *taxed* at your marginal tax rate.

For this reason, it's best to see an accountant and get an understanding of the tax implications before you make any investment choices.

Work your financial muscle on a regular basis

We haven't come from families with great wealth.

We've both worked hard and **SMART** to get where we are. We've emphasised SMART for a reason.

Working for your money isn't the best way to achieve financial fitness. *Having your money work for you* is a much more efficient way of achieving financial fitness.

Don't get us wrong, generally, you need to be doing something during the week that earns you money, so you can live the lifestyle you want. We're talking about what you do with your *surplus* funds, the funds you are depositing into your FinFit account on a regular basis.

Clearly, leaving that money in your zero to low interest-bearing account isn't going to cut it.

Let's give it a little more of a workout to get more of a result.

This is how we make our money work SMART.

The wonders of compound interest…your money works for you!

Compound interest is essentially earning interest on interest.

Albert Einstein summed it up perfectly:

"Compound interest is the eighth wonder of the world. He who understands it, earns it…He who doesn't…pays it."

How does it work?

If you made an initial investment of $5,000 and left it in the investment for 10 years, and the investment return was 7 percent per year, and you reinvested the investment return each year, your investment would look like this:

	Investment Return	Value of Investment
After Year 1	$350	$5,350
After Year 2	$375	$5,725
After Year 3	$401	$6,125
After Year 4	$429	$6,554
After Year 5	$459	$7,013
After Year 6	$491	$7,504
After Year 7	$525	$8,029
After Year 8	$562	$8,591
After Year 9	$601	$9,192
After Year 10	$643	$9,836

You can see that the amount of interest you earn each year increases because you are earning 7 percent on the previous year's investment value. You're earning *interest* on *interest*. That is why they call it *compound interest*.

The important part of this is that you need to keep reinvesting the interest you earn back into the investment. **Don't** take it out.

Compounding, and staying in an investment over the longer term, is what will help you generate wealth.

We aim to stay in an investment for a minimum of 10 years, so we can use the effect of compounding to our advantage.

What if I added extra funds to the investment each year?

Let's say you had a spare $500 a month to add to this investment. To keep things simple, let's assume the interest compounds annually. In this case, you start with $5,000 and deposit another $6,000 per year into the investment each year for 10 years. You're still earning 7 percent per year.

Your investment will now look like this:

	Investment Return	Additional Investment	Value of Investment
After Year 1	$770	$6,000	$11,770
After Year 2	$1,244	$6,000	$19,014
After Year 3	$1,751	$6,000	$26,765
After Year 4	$2,294	$6,000	$35,058
After Year 5	$2,874	$6,000	$43,933
After Year 6	$3,495	$6,000	$53,428
After Year 7	$4,160	$6,000	$63,588
After Year 8	$4,871	$6,000	$74,459
After Year 9	$5,632	$6,000	$86,091
After Year 10	$6,446	$6,000	$98,537

At the end of 10 years, you'll have $98,537 in your investment. You've deposited $65,000 into your investment account and you've made $33,537!

At 20 years, you'll have $282,539 in your investment. You've deposited $125,000 into your investment account and you've made $157,539!

If this is so great, why isn't everyone doing this?

We often ask each other this question.

The answer is that most people don't have the discipline and patience to make their money work for them.

What do we mean by this?

Firstly, the discipline—they need to have money going into their FinFit account on a regular basis, and they need to make sure they don't use it for any purpose other than getting themselves financially fit.

Secondly, the patience—they need to let time run its course. Five years, 10 years, 20 years, is a long time for most people. Human beings want instant gratification; it makes us feel good *now*. Most people struggle with the concept of having to wait years to receive their "payday." This is why people buy lottery tickets; they want the payday *now*. Statistically, you'd have more money in 20 years if you save the money you would have spent on lottery tickets rather than hoping you'd actually take home a win in the same period.

You can achieve long-term financial fitness by starting an investment plan and adding to it on a regular basis for a long period of time.

You might not have heard of John Stephen Akhwari. Type his name into Google and you'll see who we're talking about. He represented Tanzania in the marathon at the 1968 Summer Olympics in Mexico City, and he cramped up during that race because his body wasn't dealing well with the high altitude well. At the 19K mark of the race, he was jockeying for position with other runners when he fell, dislocating his knee, and hit his shoulder hard against the pavement.

He didn't stop. He got medical attention and continued the race, and he finished the race more than an hour after the winner, limping across the line.

After the race he was asked why he carried on.

His response was:

> *"My country did not send me 5,000 miles to start the race. They sent me 5,000 miles to finish the race."*

When you start a "race to financial fitness," you may encounter obstacles. These obstacles may even be considered big enough for you to give up.

Don't. Keep at it.

Your biggest obstacle could be the global stock markets. Unfortunately, they don't just steadily go up. They sometimes drop in value and they can drop big.

I want to buy my own home

It's the great Australian dream to own your own home.

We consider the following to be good reasons why you would buy your own home:

- It's forced savings. You are putting your own money into repaying your loan. As you repay your loan, you are growing your equity along the way. If you were renting, you'd be repaying the landlord's loan and helping them grow their equity.
- House prices tend to increase over the long term. Again, you are growing your equity along the way in your home. If you were renting, the landlord would be getting the benefit of the growth in equity over the long term.

We've mentioned "equity" above. We'll explain more about this concept later.

There are also the emotional reasons around owning your home versus renting. It's *your* place, and you don't have to deal with a landlord each time you want to do something to your home.

Most people will need to borrow money to purchase their own home, but how much can you borrow?

CASE STUDY:
JAMES AND HOLLY WANT TO BUY THEIR OWN HOME

A good place to start for them is to work out how much they can borrow. They go onto the FinFit lending website (www.finfitlending.com.au) and input their details into the borrowing capacity calculator.

They have one dependent, Sarah, who is three years old. They have a combined household after-tax income of $104,000 a year. James works full time, and Holly works part time. They assume a rate of interest on the home loan of 4 percent with a loan term of 30 years. They have a car loan with repayments of $300 per month, and they have a credit card with a limit of $8,000. Their borrowing capacity results are shown below.

Borrowing Power Calculator

Enter your income details

Joint Income		Yes	No
Dependents	0	1	2	3+
Net salary	$74,000	Annually	
Net salary2	$30,000	Annually	
Other net income	$0	Monthly	

Enter your expense details

Annual expense		$33,196
Car loan repayment	$300	Monthly
Other payments	$0	Monthly
Total credit card limits		$8,000

Enter your loan details

Interest Rate	4%
Loan Term	30 years

View your results

You can borrow up to	$766,000
Monthly Repayment	$3,657.00
Fortnightly Repayment	$1,687.85
Weekly Repayment	$843.92

Loan Balance Chart

Loan Balance ■ Total Payment

The calculator indicates they can borrow approximately $766,000 and the monthly loan repayment is estimated to be $3,657.

This gives them an estimate only, but it's a good guide for them to start with.

We strongly suggest that, **before you buy**, you go to see a mortgage broker who can get you a preapproval with a bank. You want to have some assurance that you can secure a loan before you commit to your purchase.

You need to be aware that every bank has a different way of assessing borrowing capacity. This means that your borrowing capacity could be different with different banks.

James and Holly now have an important decision to make.

Can they afford to pay the estimated loan repayments?

They've looked at their spending plan, and they are more comfortable with paying $3,100 a month in repayments rather than $3,657 a month. This means they can borrow only $650,000.

James and Holly decide that they want to buy a house for their growing family. They want to have another child, so they want a house that will let them raise a larger family. Based on the research they've done, the purchase price of their new home would be approximately $750,000.

Is there anything else James and Holly need to consider when buying their own home?

They need to factor in the costs associated with buying their own home.

These are:

- Loan setup costs
- Stamp duty
- Legal fees
- Lenders Mortgage Insurance

Loan setup costs are payable to the bank from which you're securing your loan. These costs can be anywhere from zero dollars to $1,000.

Stamp duty is a one-off tax levied by each state or territory in Australia on property purchases. Each state or territory uses different formulas to work out this amount. For example, if James and Holly lived in Queensland, the stamp duty on a $750,000 purchase would be approximately $19,600. If they lived in South Australia, it would be approximately $35,080.

You can find a stamp duty calculator if you go to our "Calculators" page on our www.finfitlending.com.au site.

Legal fees are paid to a solicitor or conveyancer to organise the relevant documents and formalise the transfer of the property you are purchasing into your name. These fees can be anywhere from $750 to $2,000.

The banks use the "loan to value ratio" to determine if there is any Lenders Mortgage Insurance to be paid.

The calculation for the loan to value ratio is:

The total of the loans secured against the property divided by the property value.

Lenders Mortgage Insurance is a one-time premium that you pay to the bank if your loan-to-value ratio is more than 80 percent.

This premium protects the bank, not you, if you default on the loan.

If you Google "Lenders Mortgage Insurance calculator," you'll find a calculator you can use to work this out.

James and Holly are borrowing $650,000 so their loan to value ratio will be 86.67 percent. They will incur a Lenders Mortgage Insurance premium of approximately $10,205.

Let's assume James and Holly live in Queensland, and their loan setup costs will be $200 and their legal fees will be $1,000.

Here's their situation:

Estimated home purchase price	$750,000
Estimated stamp duty and other fees	$22,000
Estimated loan setup costs	$200
Estimated legal fees	$1,000
Estimated Lenders Mortgage Insurance	$10,205
Total funds needed to purchase their home (a)	**$783,405**
Amount they are happy to borrow (b)	**$650,000**
Cash they need (a) minus (b)	**$133,405**

James and Holly need to save $133,405 to buy their own home.

They can avoid paying the Lenders Mortgage Insurance if they save 20 percent of the purchase price of the property. This means they will only need to borrow 80 percent of the purchase price and the bank won't charge them the Lenders Mortgage Insurance. In their case, they would need to save another $50,000.

Using your home to get financially fit

Your own home doesn't generate any income for you like an investment property does. You don't receive any rent. But there are ways you can you use your home to help you get financially fit.

We mentioned the concept of "equity" earlier, but what does that mean? The equity you have in your home is the difference between the value of your home less the amount of debt you have secured against your property.

To illustrate:

The value of your home (a)	$750,000
Less the value of loans secured against the home (b)	$500,000
Total Equity: (a) minus (b)	**$250,000**

You can use this equity to invest with by taking out an investment loan for the amount of equity you're comfortable using.

Comfortable is the key word here. You need to make sure you can afford to borrow the extra.

We mentioned earlier that if the loan to value ratio is more than 80 percent, you will incur Lenders Mortgage Insurance. To avoid this premium when you want to use the equity in your home, the new investment loan you take out plus the existing debt secured against your home needs to be 80 percent or less of the value of your home.

To explain:

The value of your home	$750,000
80 percent of the value of your home (a)	$600,000
The value of loans secured against the home (b)	$500,000
Usable Equity: (a) minus (b)	**$100,000**

The "Usable Equity" would be the value of your new investment loan.

This strategy is not for the fainthearted. If you're still unsure about how you can get this to work for you, get professional help. Visit FinFit.com.au/resources for more information.

You've got your financial muscle working for you, but what happens if you get injured?

You should now:

- Understand the importance of taking the right level of investment risk.
- Have an idea of the type of assets you can invest in.
- Understand that starting any financial fitness investment plan and adding to those investments over the long term will put you in a better financial position than doing nothing.

Let's now look at what you need to consider in order to prevent financial injuries from derailing your financial fitness plan.

CHAPTER 8

Don't let the unforeseen ruin your dreams and aspirations

While it is important to grow your wealth,
it is equally important to protect it.

Sport and injuries go together.

If you play for long enough, there is a high probability you are going to get hurt.

A good athlete knows that, and they will put strategies in place to prevent an injury from taking them out of the game.

Fitness and strength work will reduce the chances of injury.

A rugby league player spends a lot of time in the gym building up their strength and a lot of time on the training field building up their fitness. This helps prevent injuries. They want to be able to take big hits and play for 80 minutes at high intensity.

We're passionate about creating wealth but we're even more passionate about protecting it.

We've both been exposed to the stress and trauma caused to loved ones when death and major illness strikes.

Phil's father passed away at the age of 52 from a heart attack. He was the major income earner in the family and his mum had never worked as she she devoted her life to raising her four children. Phil was only 10 years old. His older siblings were 27, 23 and 21. There was added pressure on Phil's older siblings to work and provide income for the family. Sadly, there was no personal insurance to rely on to help during this time.

Donna's mum, Kaye, was diagnosed with cervical cancer at the age of 45 and was told it was inoperable. She went through six weeks of chemotherapy and radiation treatment. As she was recovering, Donna's stepfather, Darcy, was diagnosed with bowel cancer at the age of 57. He went through treatment and recovered only to be then diagnosed with lung cancer two years later. Darcy had a third of his lung removed and further treatment. He had two more good years before his cancer returned for the third time and he passed away at the age of 64.

Kaye and Darcy owned and ran a farm in a country town called

Yandaran (30 minutes from Bundaberg Queensland). They had seven years of cancer between them and had the added stresses of living through a drought at the same time. It's hard to imagine the pain and suffering they were going through emotionally and financially as they were living through this.

Unfortunately, they didn't have any personal insurance in place to help them financially. They both had to work in between treatments to pay the bills.

This is why we're both so passionate that our clients and their families are fully protected.

Personal insurance can be a hard topic for conversation and an extremely emotional one.

What strategies are you going to put in place to prevent injuries from derailing your financial fitness plan?

After reading this chapter, you should:

- Understand the value and importance of personal insurance.
- Have a strategy to make sure that you and your family can live comfortably if something were to happen to you.
- Understand the options you have to fund your insurance premiums.

Most people have their financial injury prevention priorities all wrong!

Eighty-three percent of Australian car owners insure their car but only 31 percent insure their income. *(www.lifewise.org.au)*

When we first raise with clients the questions around family protection and putting insurance in place we get the following responses:

1. Nothing will ever happen to me.
2. The premiums are too expensive.
3. I think I have insurance cover in my Superannuation.

The irony of these responses is that you can provide the same reasoning as to why you wouldn't insure your home or your car.

You are insuring against a probability that something may happen but the consequences are vastly different.

The right protection for the right situation

An athlete's career doesn't last forever. What's worse is that it could end prematurely with a major injury.

An important element of financial fitness is to make sure that any illness or injury you suffer is not going to stop you and your family from achieving your financial goals.

Some athletes wear equipment to protect themselves. They wear a type of equipment appropriate for the sport they play.

A tennis player won't wear a helmet when they play. They are very unlikely to be hit in the head with a tennis ball. They are more likely to have strapping around their ankles to help prevent injury.

A batsman in cricket won't wear a bicycle helmet when going out to bat. A batsman's helmet has a face guard to protect their jaw if they get hit by the ball. The bike helmet doesn't have a face guard.

The protective equipment is a form of "insurance" that will protect the wearer and allow them to keep playing if they get hit.

Your personal insurance policies offer the same protection. If something happens to you, then you and your family can still achieve your financial goals.

How do I prevent financial injury?

There are essentially four scenarios where you need protection to prevent injury to your financial goals and the financial goals of your family.

They are:

1. Suffering a major illness
2. Suffering a temporary disablement
3. Suffering a total and permanent disablement
4. Your death

Not having the right level of insurance coverage can have significant consequences.

Incorrect structuring of the policy can prevent you or your family from having a successful claim. You also need to consider carefully how you will fund the insurance premiums. You have an option to fund your premiums within your Superannuation Fund or from your personal cash flow.

Let's look at each scenario and what you need to consider when putting some protection in place.

Suffering a Major Illness...

What are the odds?

Cancer - One in two Australian men and one in three Australian women will be diagnosed with cancer by the age of 85 *(Facts & Figures - Cancer in Australia 2012, Cancer Council 2012)*.

Prostate Cancer - Around 19,400 Australian men are diagnosed with new cases of prostate cancer every year, and around 3,000 men die from it *(Prostate cancer related statistics, Prostate Cancer Foundation of Australia 2007)*.

Breast Cancer - One in eight Australian women will develop breast cancer *(Breast Health: What is breast cancer, Pink Ribbon Appeal 2008, National Breast and Ovarian Cancer Centre, National Breast Cancer Foundation 2008)*.

Heart Attack - Each year, around 55,000 Australians suffer a heart attack. This equates to one heart attack every 10 minutes *(Data and Statistics, Heart Foundation, 2012)*.

Generally, cancer, heart attack, and stroke are the three main causes of major illness. Your insurance policy can cover many other conditions related to the heart, nervous system, body organs, blood disorders, and others.

Don't underestimate the situation you may be in, and don't think your private health insurance will come to the rescue. It may not.

The good news is that, with the advancement of medical science, you've got a higher survival rate than your parents or grandparents had. As an example, cancer survival rates are increasing for most types of cancer, with five-year relative survival rates for all cancers at 66 percent *(Cancer in Australia, an overview December 2012, Australian Institute of Health and Welfare).*

The bad news is that you're left with significant lifelong medical costs to manage your condition.

In the event you suffer a major illness, you need to put your family in a comfortable financial position by:

- Providing funding for your medical and rehabilitation needs.
- Taking some time off work to focus on getting better.

You're going to have a tough time emotionally, why not remove the financial stress from the situation?

The most common names for this insurance are trauma cover or critical illness cover.

Suffering a Temporary Disablement...

How much do you rely on your income?

Assuming you were unable to work because of illness or injury, how long do you think you could survive on a zero income before needing to sell your assets?

Research showed that a significant proportion (38 percent) of working Australians could survive less than one month without their income before needing to sell assets. For under thirty-fives, this proportion was around half *(Zurich Misinsurance whitepaper February 2014).*

What are the odds?

Injury or Poisoning - Over 39,000 people will be hospitalised due to injury or poisoning this year. *(Australia's Health 2010, Australian Institute of Health and Welfare 2008).*

Depression - One in four women and one in six men suffer from depression at some time in their life *(The Victorian Government's Better Health Channel website, 'Depression – an overview', 2007).*

Disability - You have more than 60 percent chance of being disabled for one month during your working life and a one in three chance of being disabled for more than three months *(Interim Report of the Disability Committee, Institute of Actuaries of Australia 2000).*

This isn't a "career ending" injury, but it will sure make a dent in the family finances if you don't have the resources in place to get you back in the field.

The good news is that you can recover from a temporary disability and you'll be working your job and working out in the future, but...

The bad news is that without any protection, you have no income during your time off. You might be able to cash in on sick leave, annual leave, or long service leave that you have saved but that may not be enough.

If only Donna's mum and stepfather had known about this type of insurance and had a policy in place, then they wouldn't have had their seven years of financial stress on top of all the physical and emotional pain.

In the event of your temporary disablement, you need to put your family in a more comfortable financial position by making sure your income continues so you can provide for your family and cover your living costs.

The average income in Australia, at the time of writing this book, is approximately $84,000 per year before tax. Over a 35-year working life, that is a total earning capacity of $2.94 million.

Why wouldn't you want to protect that?

What is more valuable?

YOUR CAR VS YOUR INCOME

Cost -$45,000
Value in 5 years time?

Annual value now?
Value over 5 years time?
Value until you retire?

Cost to insure
$100 per month
(Illustrative only, based on popular four door sedan, major insurer, suburban Sydney, 35 year old male driver, 2014.)

Cost to insure
2% of income (before tax)
(Approximate only, individual cost varies by many factors including age, occupation and benefits chosen.)

You need income protection cover, or salary continuance cover. In the event of your temporary disablement, the insurer will generally pay you a percentage of your gross (before-tax) salary for a specific period.

Most policies will cover up to 75 percent of your before-tax income and will have a waiting period between 14 days and two years. The most common waiting period we recommend, based on our client's needs, is a waiting period of 30 days.

To work out your waiting period you need to establish what you have available to you. These are:

1. How much you have in your Emergency account.
2. The number of sick leave days you have.
3. The amount of accrued annual leave you have.
4. The amount of long service leave you have.

The policy will also have a benefit period which is the maximum length of time the insurer will pay your benefit when you're on claim. This could be anywhere between one year and until you reach the age of 70.

When determining how long a benefit period you should choose, you really need to answer the following question:

> *"Based on my current financial situation, how long will I need my income to be paid to me?"*

The most common benefit period we recommend, based on our client's needs, is a benefit period to age 65.

You also need to be aware that the benefit paid to you is a before-tax amount. You'll have to set aside any tax you need to pay. If you've structured your income protection to be paid from your Superannuation, the trustee of the Superannuation Fund is obliged to deduct any tax payable from your claim payment. If you've structured it outside Superannuation, tax will not be deducted from your claim payment.

Suffering a Total and Permanent Disability...

Total and Permanent Disability Insurance (TPD) is designed to help take the pressure off you financially if you suffer an illness or injury that leaves you totally and permanently disabled.

What are the odds?

Stroke - Stroke is a leading cause of long-term disability in adults *(The Victorian Government's Better Health Channel website, Depression – an overview, 2007)*.

Back Problems – Of those with a disability due to back problems, 44 percent are permanently unable to work *(Australian Institute of Health and Welfare, 2016. Impacts of chronic back problems. Bulletin 137. Cat. No AUS 204. Canberra: AIHW)*.

If you're a rugby league fan you might remember Newcastle Knights player Alex McKinnon whose career was cut short by a spinal injury suffered in a 2014 National Rugby League Premiership match.

He was only 22 years old when it happened.

In the Round 3 match against Melbourne at AAMI Park, McKinnon was injured in a dangerous tackle close to halftime with Storm players Jordan McLean, Jesse Bromwich, and Kenny Bromwich. Alex suffered fractures to his C4 and C5 vertebrae and was admitted to The Alfred Hospital and placed in a medically-induced coma.

Alex was left a quadriplegic.

We can't even imagine the emotional pain his family, and his girlfriend, Teigan, were going through.

The cost of his care has been significant and will continue to be so over the long term. It could be as much as $150,000 a year. This doesn't include the loss of his potential income he could have earned in the future.

People with disabilities have extra living costs that people without disabilities don't have. They have higher medical expenses and they may need personal assistance or assistive devices, such as a wheelchair or hearing aids. They may need to spend more on transportation or modified housing, and they may be restricted in what neighbourhoods they can live in to be closer to work or accessible services.

Your health and financial situation should not be a burden on yourself and your family.

In the event of your total and permanent disablement, you need to put your family in a comfortable financial position by:

- Paying off some or all your debt.
- Providing funds for your medical and rehabilitation, and ongoing care needs.
- Providing funds to help feed, clothe, and educate your children.
- Providing funds so you can continue to put food on the table.

As mentioned, the insurance policy you need is total and permanent disablement insurance, commonly referred to as TPD Insurance. In the event of your TPD, the insurer will generally pay a lump sum benefit to you.

When claiming on your TPD Insurance, you are assessed against the occupation definition set against your policy. You have two choices of occupation definition when you apply for your TPD Insurance. They are "any" occupation or "own" occupation.

"Any" occupation covers you if you are unable to return to the workforce in any occupation that is suited to your education, training, or experience.

"Own" occupation covers you if you are unable to work in your own occupation or profession (i.e. the job you have currently been working in).

Generally, the "own" occupation definition has a greater chance of a payout when you make a claim, but it can be a more expensive cover than one with an "any" occupation definition.

Most of the time we recommend an "own" occupation definition to our clients when applying for TPD Insurance.

Your Death...

This is the worst of all. Life insurance will give your family financial assistance should the worst happen.

It's staggering to think that over 95 percent of Australians do not have adequate levels of personal life insurance *(LifeWise/NATSEM study, 2010).*

Your family will be suffering enough emotional pain with your loss so it's important that they are not suffering financially as well.

If you're the main income earner, with a partner, two kids, and a mortgage, and you die unexpectedly, what position will your family be left in?

Your partner would need to find work to replace your income. Depending on the age of your kids, your partner would need to pay for the care of the kids whilst they are working. Your partner may even need to sell the house as they may not be able to fund the mortgage payments with the income they are bringing in.

Don't leave your family in a bad financial position if something happens to you.

In the event of your death, you need your family to be in a comfortable financial position by, for example:

- Paying off some or all your debt.

- Providing funds to look after your spouse or partner.
- Providing funds to help feed, clothe, and educate your children.

The insurance policy you need is Life Cover. In the event of your death, the insurer will generally pay a lump sum benefit to the beneficiary of your policy.

Funding your insurance premium

You've got a few considerations when deciding what your premium funding options are.

Some of the considerations that will influence your decision are:

- Can you afford to pay the premium from your personal cash flow?
- The type of insurance policy you want to put in place.
- The tax deductibility of your premium.

The table below gives you an overview of your funding options.

Insurance Cover	Where can I pay for my premiums?	Will my premiums be tax deductible?
Life	Superannuation	Yes
Life	Personal cash flow	No
Total & Permanent Disablement	Superannuation	Yes
Total & Permanent Disablement	Personal cash flow	No
Income Protection	Personal cash flow	Yes
Income Protection	Superannuation	Yes
Trauma	Personal cash flow	No

You should go to see a specialist who can help you decide where the best place is to fund your premiums.

Your Superannuation Fund may have insurance cover attached to it

If you have a Superannuation Fund, there is a high chance you have insurance cover in it.

Check your statement!

"I didn't apply for insurance cover in my Super Fund!!??" We hear you shout.

You're right, you didn't. They went ahead and gave you some when you joined. They gave you "default" insurance cover.

This "default" cover in your Superannuation Fund is calculated on a "unitised" basis.

What is "unitised" cover?

The amount of insurance cover you have is based on a "per unit basis" and will change with your age.

The following table gives you an example of what unitised cover may look like. We extracted this information from the First State Super personal insurance guide dated 1 October 2018. The table shows the amount of one unit of default cover you will have, based on your age.

Age of member (years)	Basic Plus (Life & TPD)
15-24	$129,190
25	$129,190
26	$129,190
27-35	$129,190
36	$127,143
37	$125,992
38	$123,562
39	$120,875
40	$112,561
41	$105,296
42	$91,527
43	$82,242
44	$72,956
45	$63,671

You can see that between the ages of 15 and 35, the insurance cover stays steady at $129,190. However, when the member reaches age 36, the cover decreases and continues to decrease as they get older. The cover will eventually cease at age 70.

Every Superannuation Fund offers different default unitised cover. You need to check the relevant "Insurance Guide" of your Superannuation Fund to see what it is.

What you need to work out is whether this "default" cover is adequate for your situation.

Remember, you didn't apply for this insurance cover. It's at the insurer's discretion whether they will pay you a benefit because you didn't undergo any medical underwriting before your insurance cover was put in place.

Because of this, the insurance policy may have a "pre-existing condition" clause attached to it.

A pre-existing condition is an illness or injury where the signs or symptoms existed before the date that your insurance cover began. If your claim is related to your pre-existing condition, then the insurer is well in their rights not to pay you the benefit.

Medical Underwriting

Underwriting is the process an insurer takes in assessing whether to accept a policy for a customer and what conditions and pricing will be applied to the policy based on medical and lifestyle information provided by the applicant.

Think of this as a kind of "fitness test." If your coach and medical staff want to make sure you get through a game playing your best, they will put you through a fitness test.

The insurer goes through a similar process to determine the outcome of your insurance application.

When you apply for insurance, you fill out your application and provide a health statement, which informs the insurer of your medical history.

The medical underwriting is done upfront when you apply for your insurance cover.

One of four things could happen after providing your medical history:

1. You have no medical issues and you will be accepted at standard premium rates.

2. You have a medical condition, which will result in the insurer applying a loading on your premiums. Examples of this are being a smoker or having an unacceptable body mass index. This could result in the premiums being increased by 50 percent to 150 percent.

3. You have a medical condition which will result in the insurer applying a medical exclusion. An example of this is back and joint issues. If they are deemed of concern by the insurer, they may exclude any claims directly or indirectly related to these issues, but still cover you for other medical conditions.

4. You have too many medical issues that the insurer is uncomfortable with and they may decline your application completely.

The advantage of going through the medical underwriting upfront is that you notify the insurer of any medical issues at the time of application rather than at the time of claim.

This will speed up the claims process, as the insurer doesn't need to go through your medical history because you've disclosed it all upfront.

The other advantage is that once the insurance policy is in place, any health issue that you have after the start date of the policy will not impact any claim.

You have a duty of disclosure…now's the time to be honest.

You wouldn't lie to your coach, would you? If you're coming into a game with an injury, they would want to know about it. They want to put the best team on the field to give everyone the best chance of victory. Hiding an injury and playing below your best will increase the chance of the team losing, and you could get dropped next week for not being a team player.

When you apply for your insurance and undergo medical underwriting upfront, you disclose your medical history to the insurer.

In simple terms, if you've ever seen a medical professional or visited a hospital for any medical condition, you need to disclose the details of this medical condition.

If it's on a medical report somewhere, disclose it!

Why? If you attempt to claim on your insurance and you didn't disclose important information to the insurer at the time of application, they are well in their rights to decline the claim due to nondisclosure.

You're probably thinking, "Even if I do disclose it, they will still decline my claim if my claim is related to the medical condition."

Not necessarily, the insurer will still assess the claim and may still pay your benefit.

It is always better to be upfront and honest with the insurer.

Doesn't Medicare and private health insurance cover me for all this?

No. They don't.

The basics of Medicare are:

- It provides universal health insurance that delivers affordable, accessible, and high-quality health care for citizens and permanent residents.
- It is provided by the Australian Government and they fund it by charging income earners a Medicare levy. Nothing is really for free!
- It assists in providing services if you need medical attention in the public system.
- It won't help you financially if something happens to you and you can't work, or you die.

The basics of private health insurance are:

- It will give you more health care options and will cover items not covered by Medicare.
- The premiums are paid by you, and the policy is provided via a private health insurance provider.
- It assists in funding services if you need medical attention, dental work, chiropractic care, or physiotherapy.
- The Australian Government will give you an income tested rebate on your private health insurance premiums as an incentive to take out private health insurance. If your income is above the highest tier, you won't get a rebate.
- It won't help you financially if something happens to you and you can't work, or you die.

Be aware of the catch...it will cost you money if you don't!

If you don't take out private health insurance and your income is above the base tier, the Australian Government will charge you an additional Medicare levy surcharge above the standard Medicare levy.

You need to assess whether or not you should take out private health insurance. It comes down to:

1. Are you going to use the services subsidised by private health insurance?

2. If you aren't going to utilise the services offered by private health insurance, what will it cost you to not have it? You need to work out what the extra Medicare levy surcharge will be versus what you'll save by paying for private health insurance.

Time for the hard conversation

Dedicate a FinFit Friday to talk about how you want to protect yourself and your family should something unforeseen happen.

Make sure the kids are in bed and you've poured yourself a glass of wine.

When going through each of the major events we want you to visualise that it has just happened to you.

What would happen to you and your family from a financial perspective?

What do you need to have in place so there are minimal financial stresses if the event does happen?

If you're a couple, each of you have an important role in the family whether you're working full time or looking after the kids full time.

To make it easier, here is a list of talking points to get the conversation started. Put a dollar figure next to each consideration so you can work out what funds you need to get you through. It's okay if you don't put a number against all of them, this is just a guide to help you.

Suffering a major illness

- You've just suffered a major trauma (e.g. cancer, heart attack, stroke, etc...). How much money do you and your family need as a lump sum to help you recover from this?

Consider...	
The cost of medical and rehabilitation	$
Reducing debt to free up some of your cash flow	$
Fund required for your partner to take time off work to help you through the treatment and recovery	$
Having a lump sum to celebrate life when you fully recover	$
Total	$

Suffering a temporary disablement

- If you get sick or injured and can't work, how would you and your family cope financially?

Consider...	
What percentage of your income do you need to maintain your lifestyle?	%
How many days can you last without your income?	
How many years do you need your income to last so you can maintain your lifestyle and long-term goals?	

Suffering a total and permanent disablement

- If you can no longer work, due to illness and injury, then how much money do you need as a lump sum?

Consider...	
The cost of medical and rehabilitation.	$
Reducing debt to free up some of your cash flow	$
The cost of a full-time carer	$
The cost to maintain your family's lifestyle	$
Total	$

Your Death

- How much does your family need to cope financially when you pass away?

Consider...	
Making sure your partner has enough to maintain their lifestyle	$
Funding required to look after the kids	$
Children's current and future education needs	$
Paying off some, or all, of your debt	$
The cost to maintain your family's lifestyle	$
Total	$

So how do you put all this insurance cover in place?

You've got two options:

Option 1: Do it yourself.

This is easier said than done so be prepared to do your research.

You can start with your Superannuation provider as you probably have some existing cover with them. You'll need to get a copy of their insurance guide, so you can read through what your options are for additional cover, how much it will cost and, importantly, how you go about applying for it.

If you want to use a retail insurance offering, then there are numerous insurance companies in Australia. We looked at the top five life insurance companies, by market share, on www.finder.com.au and found the following:

- TAL Group
- AIA Australia
- MLC Insurance
- AMP Group
- OnePath Australian Group

We suggest you research at least three of these companies to see if they will give you the cover you are looking for. That would mean getting a copy of each of their insurance guides and/or product disclosure statements and reading about the particulars of their insurance cover options, and asking for a quote on each of the insurance policies you want to put in place.

Option 2: Get someone who is qualified to do it for you.

This the easier option. They will do all the research for you, recommend the best insurer for your needs, and help you with the application process.

Your life insurance policies can be complex. If you are going to put insurance policies in place, we strongly suggest that you go see a specialist risk adviser or financial adviser that can help you.

Do insurers really pay claims?

The cynic in most people assumes that insurance is a waste of time and money as insurers try their hardest not to pay claims.

Ridiculous!

Here are some statistics for you.

The following information was provided to us by TAL Life Australia:

> *"In 2017, over 25,000 customers received $1.6 billion in claims—that's the equivalent of approximately $31 million a week. Of the claims paid, 60 percent helped our customers to continue living their lives while recovering from an illness or injury.*

The most common conditions that a claim was paid for were:

- *19 percent for cancer (breast cancer was the predominant category)*
- *17 percent for musculoskeletal and connective tissue diseases (including back pain and sciatica)*
- *15 percent for injuries and fractures*
- *14 percent for mental health (including posttraumatic stress and depression)*
- *9 percent for diseases of the circulatory system (including heart disease)."*

The following trauma and income protection claims were provided to us by Clearview Life:

Recently paid trauma claims:

Sex	Age	Occupation	Years in Force	Benefit Amount	Cause of Claim
Female	52	Secretary	3 Years	$354,764	Ovarian Cancer
Male	54	Fitter and Turner	1 year 11 months	$52,500	Parkinson's Disease
Female	31	Hairdresser	2 years 1 month	$150,000	Cancer
Male	27	Carpenter	1 year 1 month	$289,406	Hodgkin's Lymphoma
Female	44	Homemaker	1 year 11 months	$525,000	Breast Cancer
Male	37	Engineer	1 year 8 months	$400,000	Sever Ulcerative Colitis

Recently paid income protection claims:

Sex	Age	Occupation	Years in Force	Benefit Amount	Cause of Claim
Male	21	Ceiling Fixer	1 year 10 months	$2,812	Left thumb fracture
Female	41	Secretary	1 year 8 months	$2,625	Hysterectomy
Male	29	Electrician	1 year 5 months	$3,125	Epilepsy
Female	44	Orthodontist	5 months	$30,000	Fractured shoulder
Female	30	Childcare Worker	7 months	$3,875	Sprained ankle

In 2017, the breakdown of their claims lodged were:

- 25 percent Life Insurance
- 50 percent Income Protection
- 13 percent Trauma

- 2 percent Terminal Illness (benefit can be paid to claimant before their death if their condition is deemed terminal)
- 10 percent Other

The scary thing about these stats is that young people can suffer health issues. It's not just "elderly" that suffer.

Nobody is bullet proof!

A real life claim

We all know insurance is there in case we need it. We may never claim on it, but it certainly reduces the stress levels when we do.

Phil went through a real-life claim for one of his clients a few years ago.

He got a phone call from the client, who said that he had gone to see his doctor to get him to look at a couple of "blemishes" on his skin. His doctor told him that he had nothing to worry about.

He left it for a while but his gut feeling told him to get a second opinion.

He got his second opinion from a skin specialist, and the specialist told him he needed to get the "blemishes" cut out as soon as possible.

When Phil got the call, his client had just had his "blemishes" cut out and they were, in fact, melanoma (i.e. skin cancer).

It was a bit of a shock to Phil and he asked his client what stage of melanoma he had. His client was unsure but he said that if he had left them any longer, it could have been terminal for him.

Can you imagine the stress and the anxiety this client felt?

Phil had recommended, and put in place, a trauma policy for his client a few years before. His client wasn't aware his policy could potentially provide him a payout.

After the phone call with his client, Phil rang the insurance company and asked what information they needed to make an initial assessment on whether there was a basis for a claim on the client's trauma insurance policy. The insurance company ultimately decided there was a basis for a claim.

The claims process took about two weeks. Phil got a call from the insurer who notified him that the client's medical condition was serious enough for a full trauma payout of the client's policy!

The call to the client created mixed emotions as:

1. The client was elated that they had a full payout, which could take the pressure off him financially whilst he was going through the next five years of checks to make sure the melanoma didn't reappear; and
2. The client didn't know how to handle the fact that the insurer thought it serious enough to provide a full payout on the policy. He still had five years of checks to go through!

Fast forward to now and Phil's client has gone past his five years with no issues.

There is one important thing to note about this case. Phil's client was under 40 years of age when he claimed on his trauma insurance.

If you're thinking that claims are mainly made by "older" people, then think again. It could happen to you when you least expect it.

CASE STUDY:
SAM AND JENNY NEED A FAMILY PROTECTION PLAN

Sam is married to Jenny. They are both 35 years old and they have two children—Rex, seven, and Lily, five. Sam is the sole income earner of the family and he earns a before-tax income of $86,350 per year, which is approximately $65,000 per year after tax. Jenny is a stay-at-home mum.

Sam wants to make sure that if he dies, Jenny won't struggle to manage the home loan repayments, fund a good lifestyle for herself, and look after the kids. Likewise, Jenny doesn't want to leave Sam in a difficult financial position whilst looking after the kids and working. They want to make sure that if they die:

1. The mortgage on their home loan gets paid off; it is currently at $300,000.
2. Jenny will have what is equivalent to $50,000 per year of his after-tax income that would have been paid to age 60, so she can use it to look after the kids and maintain her current lifestyle. That means she needs 25 years of $50,000 per year.
3. Sam has some extra funds to help with the kids. They feel $20,000 per child, per year until each child reaches 18 will help.

They also know that the full balance of their Superannuation Funds can be paid out if they die. Sam has $90,000 and Jenny has $30,000 respectively in their Superannuation.

They calculate the amount of insurance they need and come up with the following lump sums:

	If Sam dies...	If Jenny dies...
Pay off the mortgage	$300,000	$300,000
Provide Jenny with $50,000 per year ($50,000 x 25)	$1,250,000	$0
Look after Rex	$0	$220,000
Look after Lily	$0	$260,000
Less his Superannuation balance	$90,000	$30,000
Total Insurance Cover Needed	**$1,640,000**	**$810,000**

They also consider the financial situation they would be in if either of them was to become disabled and needed full time care. They want to cover off on the same requirements as their death but also want some initial funding for any medical and rehabilitation costs they may incur. They feel $200,000 might be enough for this.

Again, the full balance of their Superannuation Funds can be paid out if they become totally and permanently disabled.

They calculate the amount of insurance they need and come up with the following lump sums:

	If Sam becomes TPD...	If Jenny becomes TPD...
Pay off the mortgage	$300,000	$300,000
Funding for medical and rehabilitation costs	$200,000	$200,000
Provide Jenny with $50,000 per year ($50,000 x 25)	$1,250,000	$0
Look after Rex	$0	$220,000
Look after Lily	$0	$260,000
Less his Superannuation balance	$90,000	$30,000
Total Insurance Cover Needed	**$1,840,000**	**$1,010,000**

Sam is the only income earner in the family. If his income stops, due to illness or injury, he and his family will be in a dire position.

He wants to insure the maximum amount of his income that he can, as they need as much of his income as possible to maintain the lifestyle they are living. They don't have much saved in their bank account, and he likes to use all his annual leave each year to go on holidays with the family. His current financial situation means he sees himself working until he is age 65.

Sam and Jenny decide on the following income protection cover for Sam:

	If Sam can't work...
Benefit Amount per year ($86,350 x 75%)	$64,762
Waiting Period	30 Days
Benefit Period	To age 65

They also realise that if either of them suffers a major illness, they will not have enough in savings to pay for any medical and rehabilitation costs. Medicare and their private health insurance will only cover a little of what they might need.

They believe that a trauma policy that would pay a benefit of $100,000 would cover most of what they'd need in terms of medical and rehabilitation costs for Sam.

Here's a summary of the insurance cover that Sam and Jenny need to put in place:

	Sam	Jenny
Life insurance cover	$1,640,000	$810,000
Total and permanent disablement insurance cover	$1,840,000	$1,010,000
Income protection insurance benefit cover (annual amount)	$64,762	$0
Trauma insurance cover	$100,000	$100,000

You have your financial injury prevention plan in place; what's next?

You should now:

- Have a clear strategy on how much insurance you need in place to protect you and your family.
- Understand where you can fund your insurance premiums.

Congratulations! You've got the making of your financial injury prevention plan. You just need to go out and implement it!

Now it's time to look at your long-term plan for financial fitness. Are you going to finish strong in your financial marathon?

CHAPTER 9

Your financial marathon – are you going to finish strong?

*Achieving financial independence starts
with your first pay cheque, not your last one!*

Your financial marathon is your race to financial independence.

Financial independence means you have sufficient wealth to

live on without having to depend on income from some form of employment.

Imagine that feeling, you have **sufficient** wealth, so you can **choose** whether you get out of bed in the morning to go to work or not!

It's your choice!! Pop the champagne, it's time to celebrate!

A good marathon runner will plan their race carefully and make sure they finish in good physical condition. You've all seen it. Those who've planned their race poorly don't finish. They are dehydrated and look like they need hospitalisation.

If you want to achieve financial independence, then your financial marathon needs a race plan.

After reading this chapter you should be able to:

- Determine what financial independence looks like to you.
- Set the date you want to be financially independent.
- Work out how big an asset base you need to generate the income you want.

You're at the start line

Your financial marathon starts when your first pay cheque hits your bank account. All you need is a good plan to get you to the finish line.

The finish line was commonly referred to as "retirement." We've decided to call it financial independence as most of our clients don't want to stop work completely. They want to be able to continue to work because they choose to, not because they have to.

Those that *need* to go to work need the money to put food on the table and pay the bills.

Those that *choose* to go to work can put food on the table and pay the bills without "needing" to go to work to earn money.

They go to work because they want to keep their mind and body active.

Work out what you need to do to finish the race

What does your financial independence look like?

Ours looks like this:

We want to own our home, be debt free, and have enough assets in place to generate the income we want when we want it. We love what we do, and we will continue to work for as long as we are able to. We want to travel domestically and internationally with our boys every year. Hawaii is our happy place and we plan to go once a year. Aloha!!!

We suggest you allocate a FinFit Friday to working out what your financial independence goal looks like. Hopefully you have as much fun as we did.

Visualise what it will look like for you. Write it all down.

What do you want to do? Go overseas on a holiday? Have a domestic holiday? Look after your grandkids? Socialise on a regular basis?

Next, set the date when you want to achieve it and write it down.

Is it your 60th birthday? Is it sooner?

Now that you have set the date, work out what income you want when you get there.

How much do you think you'll need every year to maintain that lifestyle?

$50,000?

$60,000?

$70,000?

Complete a financial independence spending plan. This will show you how much income you need to generate.

So what options do you have when it comes to assets you can accumulate as part of your race plan?

Superannuation will be a big part of your race plan...don't ignore it!

If you've ever had a job, or you currently have a job, you have a Superannuation account.

There's a good chance you have more than one Superannuation account.

Superannuation was introduced in Australia in the 1980s but it wasn't until 1992 that the then Labour Government introduced compulsory employer contributions.

The government recognised that our population was aging, and that at some point it was going to have a problem funding people's retirement via the Age Pension. It was going to put too much strain on the public purse (remember, the Age Pension is funded from the taxes we pay).

The government wants you to have enough in your Superannuation so it doesn't have to pay you as much from the Age Pension. They want you to self-fund your retirement.

The irony of this is that they are always changing the rules around Superannuation. It's no wonder people don't take enough of an interest in their Superannuation.

Having said that, you still shouldn't ignore your Superannuation.

Take an interest in your Superannuation well before you think you need to. We see a lot of people come to us in their fifties wanting to see whether they can do more to increase what they'll have in Superannuation when they get to their sixties.

They've wasted the last 30 plus years of opportunities to *increase* what they'll have when they want to get at it.

The first thing you should do is read your Superannuation statement. You should get one at least once a year, and some Superannuation Fund providers give you two statements a year.

Don't be intimidated by it!

Your statement will show you things like:

- What your opening balance was at the start of the period of the statement
- What your closing balance was at the end of the period of the statement
- Your investment choice and the asset allocation
- Your investment returns
- What your insurance cover is and what premiums you are paying
- Your beneficiaries
- What your employer has contributed

- What you've contributed
- The fees you've paid
- The tax you've paid
- Some may even have a projected balance of your fund when you reach 60.

When you do access your Superannuation and you are over the age of 60, the money you draw out will be tax free. That's right, tax free!

Seems like a good reason to pay attention to it.

That also seems like a good reason to contribute *more* into it than just what your employer puts in.

Educate yourself on the basics of Superannuation.

At the time of writing this book, the basics of Superannuation are this:

1. If you're working, your employer is contributing 9.5 percent of your before-tax income into your Superannuation.
2. There is a 15 percent tax levied on any contribution made by your employer to your Superannuation.
3. There is a 15 percent tax levied on any contribution made by you, from your before-tax salary to your Superannuation.
4. Any income or capital gain you make inside your Superannuation will have a 15 percent tax levied on it.
5. Any contribution you make to your Superannuation from after-tax dollars will *not* have a 15 percent tax levied against it.
6. There are *limits* on how much you can contribute to your Superannuation, in any financial year, before an extra tax will be levied on that contribution.
7. You need to satisfy certain conditions that will allow you to contribute to your Superannuation.

8. You need to satisfy certain conditions if you want to get access to your Superannuation.
9. If you are over 60 years of age and you have moved to "pension" phase with your Superannuation, you can draw a tax-free lump sum or a tax-free income from your Superannuation or a combination of both.

We wrote "at the time of writing" before going through these basics because the rules can change. They have changed countless times in the past and they will almost certainly change again in the future.

Make sure you're referencing the latest rules on Superannuation when you want to do more with it.

When can I access my Super again?

There are a few "conditions of release." You typically need to satisfy one of them to get access to your Superannuation.

The most common one is that you've reached your "preservation age" and you have ceased "gainful employment."

We're not going to get into the technicalities but your "preservation age" is a very important number. We encourage you to find out what your "number" is. It could be anywhere between the ages of 55 and 60, depending on when you were born.

Do note here that the access age for your Superannuation is different from the access age for the Age Pension.

Now, it's our belief and opinion that this "number" will change for some people. The government loves messing around with Superannuation rules and this one is almost certainly on their radar. This number will more than likely go up; we just don't know when this will happen. Your job is to keep an eye out for this change, whenever it happens.

If it does happen, then it will mean you'll have to wait even longer to get access to your Superannuation.

Should I be contributing more to my Superannuation?

There isn't a definitive answer to this question.

It really depends on how much you:

- Want to have in your Super when you can access it.
- Have in your Superannuation now.
- Can afford to spare to make the extra contribution.

To show the effect of contributing more to your Superannuation let's look at an example:

Josh is 30 years old and has $70,000 in his Superannuation Fund. He earns $80,000 per year before tax. His employer is contributing 9.5 percent per year of his before-tax income, i.e., $7,600 to his Superannuation.

If we assume his Superannuation returns 7 percent per annum from now until age 60, he will have approximately $641,262 in his Superannuation when he reaches age 60.

If Josh decides to contribute 5 percent per year of his before-tax salary, as a salary sacrifice, on top of his employer's 9.5 percent contribution, i.e., another $4,000, he will have approximately $865,227 in his Superannuation when he reaches age 60.

That's a $224,015 difference!

Clearly, contributing more to your Superannuation has its benefits.

Here's a summary of the effect on Josh's take home pay by making the above salary sacrifice into his Superannuation. He gets paid monthly.

Pay ($ pa)	With contributions	No Contributions
Before-tax salary	$80,000	$80,000
Less salary sacrifice	$4,000	$0
Less income tax + Medicare levy	$17,767	$19,147
Take-home pay	$58,233	$60,853

Josh's take-home pay will reduce by $2,620 per year, which is $50.38 per week.

So, Josh's $50 a week makes him $224,015 in 30 years' time. That's $78,000 worth of contributions that could turn into an extra $224,015. That's almost a 300 percent return!

Wouldn't you sacrifice $50 a week to achieve this? We certainly would!

Fees and investment returns.

These are two key considerations for you. All of them will affect how much you will accumulate in your Superannuation.

Most Superannuation Funds charge administration fees. All these fees are disclosed in your Superannuation Fund's product disclosure statement and are usually a fixed fee. You should familiarise yourself with them.

Here's an example:

Hostplus charges $1.50 per week, $78 per year in administration fees regardless of the balance in your Superannuation Fund. You can read this in their product disclosure statement.

You'll also have fees associated with the investment choice in your Superannuation Fund. These fees are usually a percentage-based fee so as your Super balance increases, the fees taken from your Superannuation will increase.

You shouldn't consider the investment fees in isolation. You need to look at the investment returns for your Superannuation. When your Superannuation Fund reports on its returns it presents that number *net* of investment fees, i.e., it's taken the fee out before it reports its performance.

Here's an example:

The below figures were taken from Hostplus' performance reports for five-year returns to the 30th September 2018.

Investment Option	Return before fees	Investment fee	Return after fees
Hostplus Balanced	11.13%	1.06%	10.07%
Hostplus Indexed Balanced	8.66%	0.05%	8.61%

Whilst the Hostplus Indexed Balanced pre-mix investment option is clearly cheaper, by a significant margin, it has under-performed the more expensive option.

If we ran these numbers using Josh as our example again there would be a $332,855 difference between each investment option when Josh reaches age 60.

Don't focus purely on fees, look at the return net of fees.

What other options do you have if you don't want to rely on your Superannuation?

If you want to achieve financial independence before you're able to access your Superannuation, then you're going to need to accumulate other assets.

We went through these options in Chapter 7.

CASE STUDY:
DAVE WANTS TO BE FINANCIALLY INDEPENDENT
WHEN HE TURNS 60

Dave has completed a financial independence spending plan and he's worked out that he needs $60,000 per year to maintain his lifestyle, which includes keeping a roof over his head and food on the table.

He also wants to take a holiday every year, so he allocates another $10,000 per year to his financial independence spending plan.

In total, Dave needs $70,000 per year when he reaches age 60.

Dave knows what the finish line looks like but he needs a race plan. He's not going to magically wake up on his 60th birthday and have the assets in place to generate $70,000 per year.

Let's work out Dave's race plan.

The first thing Dave needs to do is work out where he's starting from. Dave is 35 years old and he's going to run his race for 25 years.

Dave currently earns $70,000 per year before tax.

He needs to work out the value of his assets and how much debt he has.

Here are Dave's current assets and debts:

Asset	Value	Debts
Home	$700,000	$250,000
Superannuation	$90,000	$0
Offset Account	$50,000	$0
Car	$30,000	$0
Total	$870,000	$250,000

Dave knows that he needs to work out what his spending plan will be, and importantly, how much he has left over after expenses. This surplus or savings is what he's going to use to come up with his race plan.

Dave has completed his current spending plan and has worked out that he has $1,000 per month as a surplus. He's made the commitment to stick to his spending plan as he doesn't want to be disappointed when he gets to age 60 and hasn't reached his goal.

He makes a commitment to himself to deposit his surplus of $1,000 into his FinFit account.

The second thing Dave needs to work out is how much he needs when he reaches age 60 to generate $70,000 per year.

When Dave looks at his assets, he recognises his home and car aren't going to be much help at the finish line as he can't generate an income from them. However, they are important when he gets there, as he needs a roof over his head and his car will provide him with flexibility in getting around.

The financial assets he has are his Superannuation and his offset account.

He also knows that by the time he gets to 60, his home will have been paid off based on his current repayments.

When he gets to 60, he doesn't want to take too much risk with his financial assets. He also wants the balance of his financial assets to last as long as possible, as he doesn't know how long he'll need to generate his income from age 60 onwards. Statistically, based on current life expectancy forecasts, he's going to live to about 80, so he needs to make his assets last for at least 20 years.

The simple calculation of what assets he needs to have at 60 to generate $70,000 per year until he's 80 is:

Income needed per year x years to life expectancy = total financial assets needed

So, in Dave's case it is:

$70,000 x 20 years = $1,400,000 in financial assets.

What's Dave's shortfall?

He has $140,000 in financial assets now (i.e., his Superannuation balance plus his offset balance).

He needs to get to $1,400,000 in financial assets in 25 years' time.

So, he needs to create another $1,260,000 in financial assets over the next 25 years.

Can Dave just deposit his savings in a bank account for the next 25 years? Will that get him to the $1,400,000?

Dave has already worked out that if he sticks to his savings plan he can save $1,000 a month. Let's give Dave a boost and assume that he can get 2 percent per year in interest on his savings account, compounded monthly, and pay the interest back to the same account.

If he does this for 25 years, he would have saved about $471,000.

Wait a minute, what about Dave's Superannuation?

Dave has checked the age he can access his Superannuation, this is called his preservation age. He can access it at age 60 if he has fully "retired" from the workforce. This lines up nicely with his goal of being financially independent at 60.

Dave's employer is contributing 9.5 percent of his before-tax income to his Super. This is $6,550 per year, and Dave doesn't make extra contributions. Dave's Superannuation is invested in an investment which targets 7 percent per year growth over the long term. Dave is comfortable with taking this much risk with his Super.

Based on these numbers, he will have an estimated Superannuation balance of approximately $496,000 when he reaches age 60.

Putting it all together, at age 60 Dave will have:

Cash Balance	$471,000
Super Balance	$903,000
Total	**$1,374,000**

This is just short of the $1,400,000 he needs.

Dave has a few options to reach his goal, which we'll go through soon, but let's discuss the effects of inflation on his race plan.

The Inflation Effect…ignore it and you'll come up short!

What is inflation and why is it important?

The definition of inflation, as noted in Wikipedia, is:

> *"the sustained increase in the general price level of goods and services in an economy over a period of time."*

In Australia, the current rate of inflation is approximately 2 percent, based on the Australian Bureau of Statistics June 2018 quarter statistics. This means what you bought at the supermarket last year now costs 2 percent more this year

Historically, inflation has been running a little higher than this. The Reserve Bank of Australia try and keep the inflation rate between 2 and 3 percent.

The following table gives you a good picture of how much the cost of goods have increased since 1975.

	1975	2018
Average Wage	$7,618	$84,000
Loaf of Bread	$0.24	$3.00
1 Litre of Milk	$0.30	$1.51
Petrol per litre	$0.57	$1.60

Imagine paying 24 cents for a loaf of bread!

Why is this important?

Given that Dave wants to be financially independent in 2043 he needs to make sure he plans for inflation and what everything will cost in 25 years. The following table projects forward between now and when Dave wants to be financially independent in 25 years. It's using an inflation rate of 2 percent per year.

	2018	2023	2028	2033	2038	2043
Average Wage	$84,000	$92,743	$102,396	$113,053	$124,820	$137,811
Loaf of Bread	$3.00	$3.31	$3.66	$4.04	$4.46	$4.92
1 Litre of Milk	$1.51	$1.67	$1.84	$2.03	$2.24	$2.48
Petrol per litre	$1.60	$1.77	$1.95	$2.15	$2.38	$2.62

Imagine paying $4.92 for a loaf of bread!

Dave's $70,000 per year of income that he needs in 25 years' time is based on calculations he's made in *today's* dollars.

If inflation is running at 2 percent per year over the next 25 years, that $70,000 of income would need to be $115,362 per year in future dollars to maintain the same purchasing power.

That means Dave needs $2,307,240 in assets in 25 years' time, not $1,400,000.

Dave's $1,374,000 in 25 years' time will be approximately $833,600 in today's dollars.

If Dave doesn't allow for inflation in his race plan, he'll end up short of the finish line.

The Inflation rate does fluctuate. You just need to keep an eye on what inflation is doing when making decisions.

So, what should Dave do?

Dave has a decision to make. Clearly, saving $1,000 per month in his bank account and letting his Superannuation accumulate over the 25 years is not going to get him to the finish line.

What if he contributed the $1,000 per month into his Superannuation instead of depositing it in his bank account for the next 25 years?

Remember, his Superannuation is forecast to give him 7 percent per year over the next 25 years.

By contributing his $1,000 per month into his Superannuation instead of depositing it into his savings account, he'll end up with approximately $1,661,700 at age 60, which is approximately $1,008,000 in today's dollars.

What if he contributes the maximum he can into his Superannuation from his before-tax income for the next 25 years? The current maximum he can contribute into his Super is $25,000 per year, which is a combination of his employer contribution and his before-tax contribution.

He'll end up with approximately $2,070,000 at age 60, which is approximately $1,255,800 in today's dollars. He's getting close!

What if he took a little more investment risk with his Superannuation? His current portfolio is forecast to give him about 7 percent per year over the next 25 years. He has the option to move to a portfolio which is forecast to give him 9 percent per year over the next 25 years.

If he contributes $25,000 and moves to a portfolio which is forecast to return 9 percent per year, he'll end up with approximately $2,894,000 at age 60, which is approximately $1,760,000 in today's dollars.

He'll finish his race!

To summarise it all for you:

Dave's strategy...	What he's estimated to have in today's dollars at age 60...
Save $1,000 per month into his savings account	$833,600
Contribute $1,000 per month to his super	$1,008,000
Contribute the maximum he can to his super	$1,255,800
Contribute the maximum he can to his super and take more risk	$1,760,000

What if Dave doesn't want to take that much risk?

We've shown that Dave needs to take more risk with investment approach with his Superannuation to make his finish line. But if he is uncomfortable with that, he will more than likely come up short at the finish line.

Dave has a few options he needs to consider:

1. He changes his expectations of what lifestyle he wants at 60. Maybe he could live off $60,000 per year at age 60.
2. He tries to find more savings. If he could find an extra $500 per month, then he can use that to try and make up his shortfall over the next 25 years.
3. He gets a higher paying job which will give him more savings to work with.
4. He may have to work until he's 65. The extra five years of savings and contributing to his Super may get him over the line.

Other things to consider about Dave's race plan.

Whilst you can't predict the future, you need a plan that you can adapt to unforeseen circumstances.

It's like the drink stations in a marathon. Even though you may not feel thirsty, you still take a drink. Why? Because if you wait until you are thirsty, you're already in the initial stages of dehydration. A great marathon runner stays hydrated.

Dave's plan involves putting all his effort into topping up his Super. What if the government changes the rules around when he can access his Super? He needs to consider investment opportunities outside of Superannuation to increase his chances of getting to the funds he needs.

Dave should not "set and forget" his plan. He needs to regularly review it. If his Super investment is not giving him his expected return, he may need to change something. If the government changes the rules regarding his Super, he may need to change course.

There is no single race plan. Dave can get to the finish line in many ways. It all comes down to what he's comfortable with.

You have your race plan

You should now know:

- What financial independence looks like to you.
- How many assets you need to accumulate to generate the funds you need to be financially independent.
- That doing a financial marathon is a lot easier than running a real marathon!

We've gone through a lot to get to this point.

Let's give you a kick start to get you on the path to financial fitness.

CHAPTER 10

The 4-week FinFit Challenge – Your Financial High Intensity Interval Training (FHIIT)

*Obstacles are those frightful things you see
when you take your eyes off your goal. – Henry Ford*

This is where you get started. You'll be a lean, mean, FinFit machine in 4 weeks!

The 4-week FinFit Challenge will help you to create the foundation you need to get financially fit.

Have you ever done a fitness or weight loss challenge? You may have done one at the gym—with your personal trainer, through an online program, or via a book. There are so many options out there, and there are always new ones being introduced.

We have done a lot of fitness challenges in the past and tried many different ones over the years! We love the short-term focus and a breakdown of the simple things you need to do to reach your goals. It has also been an effective way for us to lose weight, build muscle, shape our bodies, and feel better about ourselves. We also love the nutrition and exercise support to help us achieve our goals.

While we have personally mastered and smashed our financial fitness goals, we have struggled over the years with our personal fitness and weight loss goals. We go up and we go down (just like a yoyo!) on the scales, and sometimes we need to do a challenge to get us back on track.

Therefore, we can relate to the fact that some clients have difficulties on their financial fitness journey. They can set awesome goals and have the ability to achieve them but may get side-tracked along the way. It's how you deal with that side-track that will shape your financial future.

Don't let one side-track snowball all your awesome work!!

To really achieve long-term financial fitness, you need to follow a plan, and if you get knocked down by a short-term obstacle, you need to get straight back up and focus, focus, focus!!

The purpose of this challenge is to help you save and make money.

Extra money means that more goes into your FinFit account, which means you are going to get financially fit faster.

A lot of what we'll describe in this challenge is detailed in Chapters 3, 4, 5, and 6. If you need to refresh your memory, go back and read these chapters again.

Here are the outcomes from each week:

Week 1 – FinFit Friday! Set your checkpoint for success and take control of your financial life by setting **C.O.R.E. goals**.

Week 2 – You'll create your spending plan and set up your spending plan gym.

Week 3 – You'll set up your system to track your performance and you'll find some real savings by negotiating with your service providers.

Week 4 – You'll set yourself up to pay your home loan off earlier and make some serious money this week.

Each week will start on a Friday and finish on the following Thursday. The reason for this is that you want to use the weekend to give you momentum. If you started on Monday, then your work week could distract you, and you might not get to anything until Friday anyway.

Week 1: Setting your agenda for each FinFit Friday and setting your C.O.R.E. goals

Your goals for this week are to:

1. Set your agenda for each FinFit Friday.
2. Set your **C.O.R.E** financial fitness goals.

You need to set your agenda upfront. You'll use this agenda for the four weeks of this challenge, and you'll go through this on every Friday of the challenge.

Once you've finished the challenge, you can then continue to use the format of this agenda for all your future FinFit Fridays.

Your agenda could look like this:

1. What was the best thing that happened to us this week? (Yay! Cheers to that!)
2. Goal update – How are we tracking?
3. How much did we save this week?
4. Did we have any obstacles? If so, what do we need to change to get back on track?
5. What's the plan for next week?

The first thing you need to do is set your financial fitness goals.

What are the *five* most important things that you want to achieve financially?

Remember, don't create a huge list of goals. You just won't have the time to dedicate to achieving all of them.

A small list of goals will give you focus.

Use our **C.O.R.E. goal** methodology to write down your goals.

C – Create your goal.

"I want to achieve XYZ by this date/time frame."

O – Obsess over your goal.

If you're not going to be disappointed if you fail to achieve your goal, then it's not a goal.

Visualise it! Find a picture that represents your goals and stick it on the wall. Set it as your wallpaper on your mobile phone.

R – Resource your goal.

What do you need to do to achieve your goal? Usually it's about *money* and how much you need to achieve your goal. It could also be about dedicating enough *time* to achieving your goal.

E – Evaluate how you are going to track the achievement of your goal.

Determine what system you are going to use to track whether you are on target regarding reaching your goal.

Always set some time aside to determine if you are on track to achieving your goal. If you're not on track, what do you need to do to get back on track?

If you're not going to achieve your goal in the time frame you've set for it, then what needs to change? More time? More money?

Week 2: Setting up your spending plan and your gym to go with it

Your goals for this week are to:

1. Create your spending plan.
2. Set up your spending plan gym.

Get your green and red highlighters and go through your last three months of bank statements and credit card statements.

Start highlighting your "had to spend it" items in green and "didn't have to spend it" items in red.

The total of your "didn't have to spend it" items is your *potential savings capacity*. It's *your* call how much of this spending you keep doing. Remember, every dollar spent here is one less dollar spent on your financial fitness.

Now it's time to put all these figures into your spending plan. You can use a spreadsheet or a notebook. Go to FinFit.com.au/resources for a copy of the Excel template that we use.

Put all your "had to spend it" items into your spending plan.

Look at your "didn't have to spend it" items and put a reduced amount for each of these into your spending plan.

The goal is to *reduce the junk spending* from your financial diet.

We understand it can be hard to quit cold turkey on these types of expenses, so reducing the junk spending rather than removing it completely is going to be a little easier for you to manage

If you spent $50 a week on coffee in the past three months, then put $25 a week into your spending plan and stick to it. Just making that choice will save you $1,300 a year on coffee!

As you become more disciplined, you can work toward removing them entirely.

You need structure to help create discipline. The discipline is what will get you financially fit.

Your spending plan gym gives you that structure.

Here's your basic bank account structure:

1. "Treadmill" account – your everyday account
2. "Cycle" account – your account for expenses that don't occur monthly
3. "High Five" account – your fun stuff account
4. "Emergency" account – your go-to account for unforeseen expenses
5. "FinFit" account – your financial fitness account

Settle on the bank you want to work with and create your accounts.

Download its banking app on your phone.

Go through the spending plan you created and allocate your expenses to your accounts.

Once you do that, automate transfers between your accounts. You don't want to manually move money between accounts, it wastes time and you may forget.

Ask your employer to do a direct transfer to each of your accounts.

If they won't do that, have your pay paid into your Treadmill account, then set up the automatic transfers from this account to your other accounts.

By the end of Week 2, you should have your bank accounts set up, and all the transfers in place and automated.

Week 3: Setting up your system to track your performance, and negotiating with your service providers

Your goals for this week are to:

1.   Setup your system to track your performance.
2.   Find some real savings by negotiating with your service providers.

This week is critical. You need to setup your tracking system.

If you track your expenses regularly, you'll be able to catch areas where you are going to overspend **before** it happens.

Here are your options:

1.   Pen and paper
2.   Spreadsheet
3.   Personal finance app

Personally, we like and use Option 3.

Technology is your friend. It will save you time. It will download the transactions from your bank account, categorise them for you, and help you see if you are sticking to your spending plan or not.

Type "personal financial app" into Google and select an app that you feel will work for you. Have a look at "Pocketbook" or "MoneyBrilliant."

Most of the apps offer a "free" version but these may not provide the functionality you want.

The "paid" version will give you all the "bells and whistles" to make life a lot easier for you.

Perhaps you want to use The FinFit Wealth Portal which is available at FinFit.com.au/resources if you want to take your financial fitness to the next level.

You'll need to spend anywhere between $10 and $45 dollars a month for one of these apps. If you've done your spending plan right, then you'll have room for this expense.

Research and read reviews on each app and pick the one you feel comfortable with.

This week is where you really start to "kick some goals."

It's time to lock in some savings.

You're going to ring every service provider you have and negotiate a better deal.

You want them to reduce how much you are paying for their service.

Here's a list of typical service providers:

- Utility Providers (Electricity and Gas)
- Internet Providers
- Mobile Phone Providers
- Health Insurance Providers
- Home and Contents insurance
- Car Insurance

The first step is to do your research. It is time to talk to Google!

For each of your current services, you want to get a quote from at least one service provider other than the one you're using—a quote that is lower than what you are currently paying for that service. (A quote from two other providers is even better.)

Once you've got that information, you can then call your current service provider and ask them to give you a better deal than what the other service provider can give you.

Remember, be confident.

Some will give you a better deal, some won't.

Week 4: Playing the interest savings game with your bank and making some serious money this week

Your goals for this week are to:

1. Review your home loan setup and credit card, and trim down the excessive interest amounts you pay to your bank or financial institution.
2. Find extra money to put toward your financial goals.

Step 1 – Lower your interest rate

Your first step is to do your research.

Compare the interest rate you pay on your home loan and credit card with rates charged by other banks and financial institutions. Find the one offering the lowest rate compared to what you are currently paying.

Note down the bank and the interest rate.

Let's start with your home loan.

Ring your bank that has your current home loan.

The discussion could go something like this:

You: *"Hi, can you please tell me the payout figure and the fees for discharging my loan?"*

The Bank: *"Thank you for calling. Yes, we can certainly help you with that. I'll transfer you to a specialist in that area."*

At this point you will be transferred to the bank's retention team who will start to work hard to keep your business.

The Bank (Retention team): *"May I ask why you are looking for your payout figure?"*

You: *"Yes, sure. I can get XYZ percent at bank ABC (use the interest rate and bank you noted down)."*

The Bank (Retention team): *"I will have a look at your loan and see what I can do."*

At this point they will generally come back with a lower rate and potentially lower fees. They may not match the rate that you quoted from the other bank but they should reduce their current rate.

This will also work if you have an investment loan.

The discussion with your credit card provider to get a reduced interest rate goes along the same lines.

Do your research and find other credit card providers that are offering lower interest rates than your current provider.

Ring them up and politely ask for a lower rate as you've found another bank who will give you a credit card with a lower interest rate.

A great tip here when negotiating a reduced rate on your home loan or credit card is to be persistent. If you don't get an interest rate reduction on your first attempt, then call back later and ask again. You should get a different person answering your call and you may get a better result.

Step 2 – Increase the frequency of your payments

We're assuming you've got some surplus cash after you've completed your spending plan. Direct some of this to your debt repayments.

If you're paying your home loan monthly, then divide that repayment by two and start paying that amount fortnightly. You may be able to change your repayment amount and frequency online, or you may need to ring your bank and ask them to change it.

If you're paying off credit cards or personal loans, setup an extra repayment on top of the normal monthly repayment to go towards paying this debt faster.

Step 3 – Attach an offset account to your home loan

If your bank only allows one offset account, then you could either link your Emergency account or FinFit account to it. You want to link an account that is going to have a reasonably consistent amount of funds in it, so you get the full benefit of offsetting.

If your bank allows you to have multiple offsets, then link all of your spending plan gym accounts to your home loan.

Okay, so we've focused on saving money, but let's also *make* some money this week!

Time to look around the house for things that you no longer use or need. Why? Because you are going to sell them!

This is a fantastic way to give your FinFit account a cash injection.

We've all got stuff around the house that we rarely use and have stashed away, or maybe it's just taking up space. A lot of this stuff is still in pretty good condition and could make someone else happy.

These could be things like clothes, shoes, furniture, and sporting equipment.

Make sure that whatever you intend to sell is in good enough condition. No one will buy it if it looks like it's about to fall apart.

You can sell your second-hand goods on sites such as eBay, Gumtree, or Facebook Marketplace.

If you've got a lot of stuff to sell, you might want to consider a garage sale.

Not only are you going to make some money, you are creating more space in your rooms and your cupboards!

You made it! Congratulations!

You 4-week warrior, you!

Well done completing the challenge!

Remember to celebrate your success for completing the challenge!

You've got some momentum now, but you need to stay focussed.

You can complete our 4-week challenge anytime and remember that it's not a one-time only challenge. You might want to take the challenge every 12 months. Each *subsequent* challenge will make sure you're on top of things; you might have let some areas slip. And repeating the challenge will keep you financially trim!

Let us introduce you to the 90-day plan.

CHAPTER 11

Your 90-Day FinFit Plan.
This will get you and keep you
financially fit

You're setting yourself up to achieve your goal, not necessarily trying to achieve your goal in 90 days.

A good coach keeps their pupil focused on what they want to achieve.

They'll work on short, specific goals that will help them to accomplish their ultimate goal.

Here are examples of some short-term goals you may want to achieve within your 90-day plan.

- Reduce your credit card balance from $21,000 to $18,000
- Review your spending plan every FinFit Friday to make sure you're not over spending
- Prepare your meals for the week, on the weekend, so you don't spend money on take away food
- Use your debit card instead of your credit card so you're spending your own money and not the banks

What if my goal has a long timeframe?

If you have a long-term goal such as paying off your home loan in 20 years, rather than 30 years, you'll need to increase the repayment to your home loan.

You've worked out that you need to deposit an extra $250 per fortnight into your home loan so you can pay it off in 20 years.

Clearly, you're not going to pay off your home loan in 90 days. But what you *are* going to do in your 90-day FinFit plan is:

1. Look at your spending plan to determine where you can find an extra $250 per fortnight to allocate to your home loan.
2. After you've worked out where the $250 per fortnight is going to come from, set up an automated transfer so that it is deposited onto your home loan.
3. Review your spending plan regularly to make sure you are not causing any problems with funding other expenses.

Your goal for the end of this 90-day plan is to be able to maintain your extra repayment on your home loan. You've essentially set the foundation to achieve your long-term goal of paying your home loan off in 20 years!

We have a goal to go on a family holiday once a year. We have this goal on every 90-day plan. Every 90 days we are checking that we are on track to save enough money to make sure we don't go into debt to pay for any of our holiday.

We go away with our boys every Christmas which would not happen if we didn't save for the trip all year.

We have a strong philosophy that we will not go on holidays if we don't have the money saved to pay for the entire trip in cash. We never go into debt to travel.

Your very first 90-day plan…don't try to do too many things all at once.

For your very first go at a 90-day plan, pick one goal and focus on getting set up to achieve it. If you try to start on all your goals at once, you may get overwhelmed and you may not accomplish *any* of them.

Go on—pick one of your goals and work out what you want to set up to achieve this goal in 90 days.

What do I do for future 90-day plans?

This is really up to you.

What you might want to do is:

1. Keep reviewing previous foundations you have set to make sure that you're still on target to achieve that goal.

2. Start working on setting a foundation for another one of your goals.
3. Add a new goal to your goal list.

Why should I keep track of previous foundations I've set?

We firmly believe that you should never set your goals and then forget about them.

Let's go back to our earlier example of repaying your home loan in 20 years.

What if interest rates change? What impact will this have on achieving your goal if rates go up or if they go down?

What if you've received a pay rise and you have more funds to repay your home loan even faster?

What if there is another bank that is offering better rates than your current bank? You could refinance, which could result in paying your home loan off faster.

Reviewing what you've done will make sure you are on track to achieving your goals.

How many of my existing goals should I add to my next 90-day FinFit plan?

By the time you get to your second or third 90-day plan, you'll have a good feeling about how many of your goals you can work on at once.

Keep in mind that you shouldn't have more than five goals on the go at any one time. We mentioned this in Chapter 4.

You can decide whether to work on one of your other goals or all of them. Just make sure you can devote enough time and energy to work on each of them. If you can't, then cut back on the number you want to work on at this time.

Success! I've achieved one of my goals. What do I do now?

Well done!

Don't forget to celebrate your success! We celebrate our success with a nice family dinner with our boys. We'll either call on Uber Eats or go to a local restaurant.

Make your next 90-day plan and include working out what other goals you will want to achieve. There will always be more goals to work on.

Achieving one goal will often lead you to create another related goal.

Your 90-day plan will help you focus on what you want to achieve. Regardless of whether your goals are short term, medium term, or long term, they are always a series of shorter goals achieved end-to-end.

If your goal is to save $12,000 in 12 months, then you need to save $3,000 every 90 days, or $1,000 every month. If your goal is to repay your home loan off in 10 years, how much will you need to repay each month to achieve that? Work it out and then check your progress as part of every 90-day plan.

Ninety days is a great length of time to create some momentum and keep you focused on achieving your goals.

CHAPTER 12

If you want to achieve financial fitness, you have to make it happen

You've been on a journey of discovery.

You've discovered that to get to peak financial fitness:

- A quick financial health check will tell you how financially unfit you are.

- FinFit Friday is your checkpoint for success. It will give you a chance to assess if you are on track to peak financial fitness.
- Setting **C.O.R.E goals** will help you take control of your financial life.
- Setting and sticking to a spending plan will help you make the right choices to get to financial fitness.
- Carrying too much financial flab (i.e. debt) is going to slow you down.
- Flexing your financial muscle by making your money work smarter for you will get you to financial fitness quicker.
- Having the right level of insurance in place will allow you to still reach your financial goals if something unforeseen happens.
- Your financial marathon, your race to "financial independence," requires a plan, and also the patience and commitment to execute it.
- Our 4-week FinFit Challenge will give you the kick start you need to get on the path to financial fitness.
- Your 90-day plan will keep you focused with your eye on the prize!

You now need to act.

Your financial fitness isn't going to improve by itself.

Don't just add this book to the other financial self-help books you have on your bookshelf.

The concepts in this book only work when they are put into practice, and we've structured this book in such a way that it makes it easy for you to take a concept and implement it.

We've removed two of the major impediments that will get in the way of you becoming financially fit, which are:

1. "Where do I start?"
2. "What should I do?"

Simple: start from the beginning of this book and implement our suggestions as you go through the book.

You will move from being financially unfit to being a lean, mean, money-making machine, and importantly, you'll stay that way.

How do I know if I've improved my financial fitness?

Remember that health check we got you to complete at the start of the book?

Redo it at least every 12 months.

Whether you're a professional athlete or someone who just wants to get physically fit, there will be times when you need to track how you are progressing. You want to know where you started from and where you are now, so you can determine whether the "activity" you are doing in between "checks" has improved your situation.

Great, my health check is telling me I'm 100 percent financially fit, so I don't need to do it anymore...

Whatever you do, don't stop improving your financial fitness!

Why? If you want to stay at peak financial fitness, you have to keep checking to see if you are still there.

If your financial goals change, you'll need to go back and review what you are doing to make sure you'll achieve your new goals. You may need to change what you are doing. If you change something, you must keep checking to make sure you're on track.

Change is constant. There will be changes in economic conditions, laws, your personal and financial situation, and many other things that can impact your financial fitness.

You need to be able to react and adapt.

Your financial fitness is either improving or declining; it won't stay static.

Thanks for reading our book. Good luck on your journey to financial fitness. Stay strong and focused, and you'll succeed.

ABOUT THE AUTHORS

Phil and Donna Sgangarella are the cofounders of FinFit Wealth Solutions. They are personal financial coaches with a passion for helping clients achieve peak financial fitness.

Phil and Donna have more than 35 years combined financial services experience.

Phil began his working life as an IT professional in 1990. He excelled in the industry for 14 years, but he was interested in helping people improve their lives; he wanted to make a real difference. He'd always enjoyed financial planning for himself, so his future direction soon became clear.

In 2004, Phil became a financial adviser, and he received a diploma in financial planning through Tribeca in 2005. In the same year, he received an advanced diploma in financial planning, and he became a Certified Financial Planner in 2008. He worked for a mid-sized financial services firm for almost 10 years, and then decided to leave and go into business with his lovely wife, Donna. Phil has helped clients succeed by listening to their concerns, and coaching them to become better money managers and wealth accumulators.

Most of Phil's clients come to him wanting more structure, discipline, and direction with regard to their financial situation. All of them now have a total understanding of their financial path. Seeing clients succeed is Phil's greatest reward. He believes in sharing knowledge to help people improve their lives, and he enjoys turning his clients' dreams into reality—one financial plan at a time.

Donna is a qualified Mortgage Broker with more than 25 years' experience in the financial services industry. She spent the first 14 years working in various roles at Westpac Bank, starting as a Westpac financial planner and then getting promoted to various roles due to her skills, expertise, and experience. These included working as a Practice Manager in New South Wales and Queensland, and then working as a Key Account Manager for clients who were using the BT Wrap platform.

Donna then decided to enhance her skills in funds management. She worked for an asset manager—Antares Equities—as a Business Development Manager, and then was promoted to State Manager, and later Head of Retail Sales in Australia.

She is passionate about financial planning, and working with people to help them achieve their goals. She understands the issues clients face, and works closely with them to help them pursue their dreams.

Phil and Donna live in Brisbane and have clients all over Australia.

They are happily married with three handsome boys—Jarrod, Rhys, and Rocco. They are together 24/7 and would not have it any other way.